Roald Dahl Short Stories

로알드 달 단편 모음

Fantastic Mr. Fox
The Magic Finger
The Enormous Crocodile
The Giraffe and the Pelly and Me

Contents

원서 읽는 단어장 소개 ·········· 4

이 책의 구성 ·········· 6

영어원서 읽기 전문가가 대답해주는 FAQ ·········· 8

The Enormous Crocodile

Comprehension Quiz ·········· 12

Build Your Vocabulary ·········· 24

The Giraffe and the Pelly and Me

Comprehension Quiz ·········· 38

Build Your Vocabulary ·········· 52

Fantastic Mr. Fox

   Comprehension Quiz · 82

   Build Your Vocabulary · 100

The Magic Finger

   Comprehension Quiz · 152

   Build Your Vocabulary · 158

Answers

   Comprehension Quiz Answers · · · · · · · · · · · · · · · · · · · 168

   영어원서 읽기 Tips · 170

원서 읽는 단어장 소개

누구나 추천하는 최고의 영어 공부법, 영어원서 읽기!

최근 영어원서 읽기가 영어 공부법으로 주목받고 있습니다. 영어를 많이 접하는 것이 영어 실력을 향상시키는 가장 바람직한 방법이라는 공감대가 형성되면서, 쉽고 저렴하게 영어를 접할 수 있는 '원서 읽기'가 그 대안으로 각광받고 있는 것이지요.

실제로도 영어 좀 한다는 사람들이 원서 읽기를 추천하거나, 어린 아이들이 엄마표 영어 연수 등을 통해 원서를 읽는 많은 사례들을 인터넷 상에서 쉽게 찾아볼 수 있습니다.

원서 읽기를 위한 최고의 친구, 『원서 읽는 단어장』!!

원서 읽기가 영어 공부를 하는 좋은 수단이긴 하지만, 한 번쯤 원서를 읽어 본 독자들은 대부분 다음과 같은 고민을 하곤 합니다.

누가 여기 나오는 단어 좀 찾아주면 안 되나?
모르는 단어가 나올 때마다 사전을 찾을 수도 없고,
그렇다고 그냥 지나치자니 뭔가 찜찜한데…

지금 내가 제대로 읽고 이해하고 있는 걸까?
번역된 책을 찾아서 일일이 대조할 수도 없고,
뭔가 확인할 방법이 있었으면 좋겠는데…

이런 문제를 해결해주고자, 여기 『원서 읽는 단어장』이 왔습니다!
원서 읽는 단어장은, 영어원서에 나온 어려운 어휘들을 완벽히 정리해서 원서 읽기의 부담감을 줄이고 보다 효과적으로 영어 실력을 쌓을 수 있도록 도와주는 책입니다. 또한 이해력을 점검하는 Comprehension Quiz를 통해 내가 원서를 정확히 읽고 있는지 확인해볼 수 있습니다.

『원서 읽는 단어장』시리즈를 통해 영어원서를 보다 쉽고 재미있게 읽고, 영어 실력도 쑥쑥 향상시켜보세요.

이 책은 Roald Dahl(로알드 달)의 대표 단편 『The Enormous Crocodile』, 『The Giraffe and the Pelly and Me』, 『Fantastic Mr. Fox』, 『The Magic Finger』 독자들을 위해 만들어졌습니다. 위 영어원서들은 시중 서점 및 인터넷 서점에서 쉽게 구입할 수 있습니다.

이 책의 구성

Comprehension Quiz

원서를 제대로 읽고 이해하고 있는지 측정해보는 간단한 퀴즈입니다.

원어민 Extensive Reading 전문가가 출제한 쉽고 재미있는 문제들로 구성되어 있습니다. 퀴즈를 풀어보고 틀린 부분이 있다면, 제대로 이해한 것이 맞는지 해당 내용을 다시 한 번 점검해봐야겠죠?

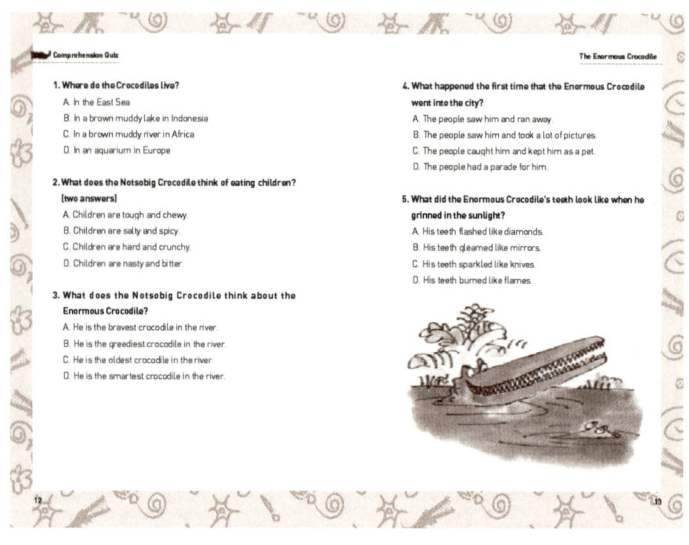

퀴즈는 각 챕터별로 약 5개 안팎의 문제가 출제되어 있습니다.

각 챕터를 읽고 바로 문제를 풀어보는 것도 좋고, 혹은 시간이 되는 대로 쭉 읽은 후 해당 부분만큼 문제를 풀어보는 것도 좋은 방법입니다. 자신의 상황과 스타일에 맞게 적절히 활용하세요!

정답은 168페이지에 있습니다.

Build your Vocabulary

원서에 등장하는 어려운 어휘가 정리되어 있습니다.

단어는 각 챕터별로, 원서에서 단어가 등장하는 순서 그대로 정리되어 있으며, [빈도-스펠링-발음기호-한글 뜻-영어 뜻] 순으로 표기되어 있습니다.

별표(★)가 많을수록 필수 어휘입니다. 또 이전 챕터에서 등장한 중요 어휘가 반복해서 나올 때는 '**복습**'이라고 표시해서 정리했습니다.

여기 정리된 단어를 일일이 손으로 쓰면서 '암기'하려고 하지는 마세요! 실질적인 어휘 암기는 원서를 읽으면서 문맥 속에서 단어와 자주 마주칠 때 이루어집니다! 단어 리스트는 원서를 읽기 전후에 눈으로 쭉 살피면서 '단어와 익숙해지도록' 만드는 데 활용하세요. 원서를 읽을 때 단어에서 오는 부담감이 줄어들고, 매우 효율적으로 어휘 실력을 향상시킬 수 있습니다.

영어원서 읽기 전문가가 대답해주는 FAQ

Q. 단어장에 나오는 단어 중에 모르는 단어가 너무 많네요. 전부 외워야 할까요?

A. 모든 단어를 완벽하게 외울 필요는 전혀 없습니다! 원서에 나오는 단어 중에는 보통 상황에는 거의 사용되지 않는 단어도 많고, 심지어 작가가 만든 단어까지 있습니다. 이런 단어들을 철저하게 외우는 것은 정말 비효율적인 일이지요.

일단 원서를 읽기 전에 단어장을 쭉 훑어봅니다. 빈도가 높고(★ 개수가 많고), 책 안에서 자주 반복되는 단어들('복습'이라고 표시되어 있는 단어들)을 우선하여 주의 깊게 살펴보세요. 이 때 모든 단어를 완벽하게 암기할 필요는 없습니다. 가볍게 눈으로 보고 바로 원서 읽기에 들어가세요. 원서를 읽으면서 방금 훑어봤던 단어를 자연히 마주치게 되고, 이런 과정에서 그 단어의 뜻은 물론 쓰이는 상황과 느낌까지 한꺼번에 학습하게 됩니다. 또 원서 읽기를 마치면 그날 읽은 부분에 나오는 단어를 한 번 더 훑어보는 것으로 마무리하세요. 이렇게 단어를 자주 마주치다 보면 어휘력을 더 탄탄하게 다질 수 있습니다.

우리는 일반적으로 단어 암기를 할 때, 눈으로 보고, 손으로 쓰고, 입으로 발음하면서, 즉 오감을 활용해서 암기하려고 합니다. 이런 방식의 암기는 매우 좋은 방법이지만, 기초 필수 어휘 외의 다른 단어 암기에도 같은 방식을 적용시키는 것은 너무 비효율적입니다. 자주 쓰이고 중요한 어휘라면 원서를 읽으면서(영어를 폭넓게 접하면서) 많이 만날 수밖에 없고, 굳이 의도하지 않아도 자연스럽게 암기하게 됩니다. 이렇게 '영어를 많이 접하면서' 어휘력을 향상시키는 것이 가장 좋은 단어 학습법입니다.

Q. 저는 말하기도 잘하고 싶은데, 원서 읽기가 도움이 될까요?

A. 물론 원서 읽기는 말하기에도 많은 도움이 됩니다!

유창한 말하기는 모든 영어 학습자의 로망이라고 할 수 있습니다. 하지만 영어 말하기를 원하는 학습자가 쉽게 간과하는 것이 있는데, 그것은 'Input이 없으면 그만한 Output도 없다'는 사실입니다.

영어 말하기는 이미 영어를 많이 접하고 머릿속에 충분한 양이 축적되었을 때에야만 자연스럽게 터져 나옵니다. 따라서 영어 말하기의 전제 조건은 일단 '영어를 폭넓게 접할 것, 영어 Input의 양을 충분히 늘릴 것'입니다. 그리고 이렇게 '영어 Input'을 폭발적으로 늘리는 가장 좋은 방법이 바로 영어원서 읽기입니다! 언제 어디서나 원서를 펴기만 하면 곧바로 영어를 접할 수 있는 환경이 만들어지기 때문이지요.

유창한 말하기를 원하십니까? 그럼 원서를 많이 읽으세요! 아직 말하기가 만족스럽지 않다면 더 열심히 읽으셔야 합니다. 원서를 읽으면서 발견하는 좋은 표현들이나 등장인물들의 대화를 큰 소리로 따라 읽는 것도 매우 좋은 방법입니다. 또 오디오북을 들으면서 성우의 발음과 억양을 최대한 흉내 내며 소리 내어 읽는 것도 추천해드립니다. 이런 노력들이 쌓이고 쌓여서 탁월한 말하기 실력으로 돌아올 것입니다.

Q. 로알드 달 단편 모음을 정말 재미있게 읽었어요! 비슷한 수준의 다른 원서 좀 추천해주세요.

A. 일단 기본적으로 같은 저자 Roald Dahl의 다른 책들을 읽어볼 것을 추천해드립니다. 같은 저자가 썼기 때문에 똑같이 재미를 느낄 수 있고, 같은 어휘와 문체가 반복해서 등장하기 때문에 자연스럽게 복습하는 효과를 얻게 됩니다. (Roald Dahl의 「Charlie and the Chocolate Factory」, 「Matilda」, 「James and the Giant Peach」 역시 「원서 읽는 단어장」으로 출간되었습니다.)

이 외에 앤드류 클레멘츠(Andrew Clements)의 책을 추천해드립니다. 그의 작품으로는 「Frindle」, 「The Landry News」 등 다양한 책이 있습니다. 원어민 초등학생을 위해 쓰인 책이긴 하지만, 남녀노소 모두 좋아할 만한 내용에 영어 수준도 무난해서 Roald Dahl의 애독자라면 꼭 한번 읽어볼 만합니다. 또한 미국의 인기 작가 루이스 로리(Lois Lowry)의 「Number the Stars」, 뉴베리상 수상작인 「Sarah, Plain and Tall」도 같은 수준의 추천할 만한 책들입니다.

The Enormous Crocodile

Comprehension Quiz

1. Where do the Crocodiles live?

  A. In the East Sea

  B. In a brown muddy lake in Indonesia

  C. In a brown muddy river in Africa

  D. In an aquarium in Europe

2. What does the Notsobig Crocodile think of eating children? (two answers)

  A. Children are tough and chewy.

  B. Children are salty and spicy.

  C. Children are hard and crunchy.

  D. Children are nasty and bitter.

3. What does the Notsobig Crocodile think about the Enormous Crocodile?

  A. He is the bravest crocodile in the river.

  B. He is the greediest crocodile in the river.

  C. He is the oldest crocodile in the river.

  D. He is the smartest crocodile in the river.

The Enormous Crocodile

4. What happened the first time that the Enormous Crocodile went into the city?

    A. The people saw him and ran away.

    B. The people saw him and took a lot of pictures.

    C. The people caught him and kept him as a pet.

    D. The people had a parade for him.

5. What did the Enormous Crocodile's teeth look like when he grinned in the sunlight?

    A. His teeth flashed like diamonds.

    B. His teeth gleamed like mirrors.

    C. His teeth sparkled like knives.

    D. His teeth burned like flames.

Comprehension Quiz

6. Why does the Enormous Crocodile think that he will be able to eat a child this time?

   A. Because he is greedy.

   B. Because he is stupid.

   C. Because he has a big mouth.

   D. Because he has clever tricks.

7. What does Humpy-Rumpy hope will happen to the Enormous Crocodile?

   A. "I hope you get caught and sent to a zoo where you will see children everyday but never be able to eat one."

   B. "I hope you get caught and made into a crocodile bag."

   C. "I hope you get caught and made into a short table."

   D. "I hope you get caught and cooked and turned into crocodile soup."

8. What does the Crocodile do to get Trunky's attention?

   A. He whistles.

   B. He stands up on his tail and looks Trunky in the eye.

   C. He bites Trunky's leg.

   D. He says hello.

The Enormous Crocodile

9. What did Trunky call the Crocodile? (two answers)

   A. You foul and filthy fiend.

   B. You wicked beastly beast.

   C. You harmful horned toad.

   D. You silly slithering serpent.

10. What does Muggle-Wump offer the Crocodile to eat?

   A. A juicy child

   B. A few nuts

   C. Another monkey

   D. A tree

Comprehension Quiz

11. What did the Crocodile do to Muggle-Wump's tree?

A. He watered it to make it grow better.

B. He shook it to get the nuts that Muggle-Wump offered.

C. He smacked it with his tail to scare Muggle-Wump.

D. He bit through the tree and knocked it down.

12. Why does the Crocodile tell all of the animals about his clever tricks?

A. He doesn't care what the other animals think about eating children.

B. He wants the other animals to think that he is smart.

C. He wants advice from the other animals on how to catch and eat children.

D. He wants to eat the monkeys and birds, so he fools them with a story.

13. What did NOT happen when the Crocodile tried to bite the Roly-Poly Bird?

A. The Roly-Poly Bird let out a shriek of terror.

B. The Roly-Poly Bird shot straight up in the air.

C. The Roly-Poly Bird left his beautiful tail feathers behind.

D. The Roly-Poly Bird said, "I am going to get revenge on you soon."

The Enormous Crocodile

14. What did the Crocodile collect for Clever Trick Number One?

  A. Clothes and a moustache

  B. Coconuts and fallen branches

  C. A lot of balloons

  D. Feathers and flowers

15. Why couldn't Toto and Mary find any coconuts on the ground?

  A. Because it was the wrong season for coconuts.

  B. Because the Crocodile had gathered them all up.

  C. Because the other children had already found all of the coconuts.

  D. Because you always have to climb a tree to pick the coconuts.

Comprehension Quiz

16. What did the Crocodile do when the children came closer to him? (two answers)

A. He licked his lips.

B. He started to shake with excitement.

C. He started to dribble.

D. He roared like a lion.

17. What is NOT true about Humpy-Rumpy?

A. He was galloping at a terrific speed.

B. His head was down low.

C. He was crashing and snorting.

D. He was tired and out of breath.

18. What happened when Humpy-Rumpy hit the Crocodile?

A. The Crocodile flew through the air.

B. The Crocodile went tumbling and skidding over the ground.

C. The Crocodile didn't move.

D. The Crocodile bit Humpy-Rumpy.

The Enormous Crocodile

19. **What did the Crocodile need for Clever Trick Number Two? Why?**

    A. A chain to pretend to be a swing

    B. A bar to pretend to be a merry-go-round

    C. A metal sheet to pretend to be a slide

    D. A log to pretend to be a seesaw

20. **What do the children NOT think of the seesaw?**

    A. It is new.

    B. It is knobbly.

    C. It is strong.

    D. It is hungry.

Comprehension Quiz

21. What is the Crocodile waiting for?

    A. For one of the children to sit on his head

    B. For one of the children to jump on his back

    C. For one of the children to hold his tail

    D. For one of the children to poke his eye

22. What food were they selling at the fair? (two answers)

    A. Elephant ears

    B. Cotton Candy

    C. Funnel Cakes

    D. Popcorn

23. What animal was NOT on the merry-go-round?

    A. White tigers

    B. Dragons with red tongues

    C. Mermaids with fish tails

    D. Hippogriffs with birds wings

24. What was the Crocodile's Clever Trick Number Three?

A. To hide in the hall of mirrors

B. To pretend to be a wooden crocodile on the merry-go-round

C. To pretend to be a clown

D. To pretend to be the train on a roller coaster

25. Before the Crocodile needed to eat three or four children, but now he needs to eat six children. Why?

A. Because he is angry.

B. Because he doesn't like the other forest animals.

C. Because he missed three chances to eat children.

D. Because he has a big mouth.

Comprehension Quiz

26. What was NOT part of Clever Trick Number Four?

A. He picked flowers and put them on a table.

B. He hid the bench in the bushes.

C. He pretended to be a bench.

D. He painted the table green.

27. What was the Crocodile thinking when the family came close? (two answers)

A. "I will eat them all."

B. "I will let them eat their picnic and go home."

C. "I will wait until they sit on my back."

D. "I will chase them before any animals can stop me this time."

28. Put the events in order: (–   –   –   )

A. Trunky trotted over to the Crocodile.

B. The Crocodile yelled "Hey! Let me go!"

C. Trunky grabbed the Crocodile's tail and hoisted him up.

D. Trunky said "No, we have all had enough of your clever tricks."

29. What did Trunky do to the Crocodile?

A. He sat on the Crocodile and squished him as flat as a pancake.

B. He swung the Crocodile like a baseball bat and hit all of the coconuts in all of the trees.

C. He swung the Crocodile around in a circle very very fast.

D. He pounded the Crocodile into the ground like a giant green nail.

30. Put the events in order: (–   –   –   )

A. The Crocodile hit the sun with a tremendous BANG.

B. The Crocodile was sizzled up like a sausage.

C. The Crocodile went shooting up into the sky.

D. The Crocodile went into space and past the moon.

Build Your Vocabulary

* **muddy** [mʌ́di] a. 진흙의; 흐린, 탁한; 흐리멍텅한
  Something that is muddy contains mud or is covered in mud.

* **enormous** [inɔ́ːrməs] a. 막대한, 거대한
  You can use enormous to emphasize the great degree or extent of something.

  notsobig (= not so big) 그렇게 크지 않은

* **grin** [grin] v. 이를 드러내고 싱긋 웃다; n. 싱긋 웃음
  When you grin, you smile broadly.

* **juicy** [dʒúːsi] a. 즙 많은, 수분이 많은; (이야기가) 흥미진진한
  If food is juicy, it has a lot of juice in it and is very enjoyable to eat.

* **paddle** [pǽdl] v. 물을 젓다, 노를 젓다; n. 라켓; 노, 패들
  If you paddle a boat, you move it through water using a paddle.

* **gulp** [gʌlp] v. 꿀꺽꿀꺽 마시다; (긴장, 흥분으로) 꿀꺽 삼키다; n. 꿀꺽꿀꺽 마심
  If you gulp something, you eat or drink it very quickly by swallowing large quantities of it at once.

  gollop 사전에 없는 저자가 만든 단어
  gulp(v. 꿀꺽꿀꺽 마시다)와 같은 뜻으로 쓰였다.

* **tough** [tʌf] a. 질긴, 차진; 튼튼한, 강인한; 곤란한, 힘든
  A tough substance is strong, and difficult to break, cut, or tear.

  chewy [tʃúːi] a. 잘 씹어지지 않는; 잘 씹을 필요가 있는
  Needing to be chewed a lot before it can be swallowed.

* **nasty** [nǽsti] a. 더러운, 불쾌한; 심술궂은, 비열한
  Something that is nasty is very unpleasant to see, experience, or feel.

* **bitter** [bítər] a. 쓴; 쓰라린, 지독한
  A bitter taste is sharp, not sweet, and often slightly unpleasant.

* **awful** [ɔ́ːfəl] a. 지독한, 대단한; 무서운; ad. 몹시
  If you look or feel awful, you look or feel ill.

The Enormous Crocodile

tommy-rot [támirɑt] n. (속어) 되지 못한 소리[생각]
Tommy-rot is silly talk or writing.

yummy [jʌ́mi] a. 맛있는; 아주 매력적인
Yummy food tastes very good.

helping [hélpiŋ] n. (음식의) 한 번 담는 분량, 한 그릇; 원조; a. 도움이 되는
A helping of food is the amount of it that you get in a single serving.

⁂ **greedy** [grí:di] a. 탐욕스러운; 열망하는 (greedily ad. 욕심내어, 탐욕스럽게)
Wanting a lot more food, money, etc. than you need.

croc [krɑk] n. (= crocodile) 악어
Croc means crocodile.

⁂ **dare** [dɛər] v. 감히 …하다; 무릅쓰다; 도전하다
If you dare to do something, you do something which requires a lot of courage.

★ **snort** [snɔ:rt] v. 콧김을 뿜다, (경멸 등으로) 콧방귀 뀌다; n. 거센 콧김[바람]
When people or animals snort, they breathe air noisily out through their noses.

⁂ **sparkle** [spá:rkəl] v. 불꽃을 튀기다, 생기가 넘치다; n. 불꽃, 광채
If something sparkles, it is clear and bright and shines with a lot of very small points of light.

⁂ **feast** [fi:st] v. 축연을 베풀다; 진수성찬을 먹다; n. 축제; 대접; 진수성찬
If you feast on a particular food, you eat a large amount of it with great enjoyment.

⁂ **crawl** [krɔ:l] vi. 기어가다, 느릿느릿 가다; n. 기어감; 서행
When you crawl, you move forward on your hands and knees.

★ **gigantic** [dʒaigǽntik] a. 거대한, 막대한
If you describe something as gigantic, you are emphasizing that it is extremely large in size, amount, or degree.

slimy [sláimi] a. 진흙투성이의, 진흙을 바른; 알랑대는, 비굴한
Slimy substances are thick, wet, and unpleasant.

25

Build Your Vocabulary

* **ooze** [u:z] v. 스며 나오다, 새어나오다; n. 스며 나옴 (oozy a. 스며 나오는)
  When a thick or sticky liquid oozes from something or when something oozes it, the liquid flows slowly and in small quantities.

* **hippopotamus** [hìpəpátəməs] n. [동물] 하마
  A hippopotamus is a very large African animal with short legs and thick, hairless skin.

  on earth idiom [의문사를 강조하여] 도대체, 어떻게
  You use 'on earth' with questions, in order to express your surprise or anger.

* **horrid** [hɔ́:rid] a. 무시무시한; 매우 불쾌한, 지겨운
  If you describe something as horrid, you mean that it is very unpleasant indeed.

  tummy [tʌ́mi] n. 배
  Your tummy is the part of the front of your body below your waist.

  grumptious 사전에 없는 저자가 합성한 단어
  grumpy (a. 성미 까다로운, 심술난) + …ious (…의 특징을 가진)

* **brute** [bru:t] n. 짐승, 야만인; a. 잔인한, 무정한
  If you call someone, usually a man, a brute, you mean that they are rough, violent, and insensitive.

  waddle [wάdl] vi. 뒤뚱거리며 걷다, 흔들흔들 거리며 가다; n. 뒤뚱거리는 걸음걸이
  To waddle somewhere means to walk there with short, quick steps, swinging slightly from side to side.

* **nibble** [níbəl] v. 조금씩 물어뜯다, 갉아먹다; n. 조금씩 물어뜯기, 한 입 분량
  If you nibble food, you eat it by biting very small pieces of it.

* **beastly** [bí:stli] a. 짐승 같은; 잔인한; 더러운, 불결한 ad. 몹시, 아주
  If you describe something as beastly, you mean that it is very unpleasant.

  crunch [krʌntʃ] n. 우두둑 부서지는 소리; v. 우두둑 깨물다[부수다]
  A crunch is a noisy crackling sound.

The Enormous Crocodile

‡ wicked [wíkid] a. 사악한, 심술궂은
You use wicked to describe someone or something that is very bad and deliberately harmful to people.

‡ foul [faul] a. 더러운, 불결한, 냄새 나는; 부정한, 비열한, 못된
If you describe something as foul, you mean it is dirty and smells or tastes unpleasant.

* filthy [fílθi] a. 불결한, 더러운
Something that is filthy is very dirty indeed.

* fiend [fi:nd] n. 마귀, 악마, 악령
If you describe someone as a fiend, you mean that they are extremely wicked or cruel.

* squash [skwɑʃ] ① v. 눌러 찌그러뜨리다; 헤치고[밀치고] 들어가다 ② n. [식물] 호박
If someone or something is squashed, they are pressed or crushed with such force that they become injured or lose their shape.

squish [skwiʃ] v. 찌부러뜨리다, 으깨다
If something soft squishes or is squished, it is crushed out of shape when it is pressed.

squizzle 사전에 없는 저자가 만든 단어
squash(v. 눌러 찌그러뜨리다)와 같은 뜻으로 쓰였다.

‡ boil [bɔil] ① v. 끓(이)다; 격분하다; n. 끓임, 삶음 ② n. 종기, 부스럼
When a hot liquid boils or when you boil it, bubbles appear in it and it starts to change into steam.

* stew [stʃuː] n. 스튜(요리); v. (약한) 불로 끓(이)다
A stew is a meal which you make by cooking meat and vegetables in liquid at a low temperature.

‡ sniff [snif] v. 코를 킁킁거리다, 냄새를 맡다; 콧방귀를 뀌다; n. 킁킁거리며 냄새 맡음; 콧방귀 뀜
When you sniff, you breathe in air through your nose hard enough to make a sound, for example when you are trying not to cry, or in order to show disapproval.

Build Your Vocabulary

pale [peil] a. 창백한; 엷은, 연한; 희미한; v. 엷어지(게 하)다
If someone looks pale, their face looks a lighter color than usual, usually because they are ill, frightened, or shocked.

gobble [gábəl] v. 게걸스레 먹다; 탐독하다
If you gobble food, you eat it quickly and greedily.

hoggish [hɔ́ːgiʃ] a. 돼지 같은; 탐욕스러운; 더러운
Something that is hoggish has the characteristics of a pig.

creepy [kríːpi] a. 소름이 끼치는; 꾸물꾸물 움직이는
If you say that something or someone is creepy, you mean they make you feel very nervous or frightened.

buckle [bʌ́kəl] n. (혁대 등의) 버클, 장식 죔쇠; v. 죔쇠로 죄(이)다; 구부리다[러지다]
A buckle is a piece of metal or plastic attached to one end of a belt or strap, which is used to fasten it.

throat [θrout] n. 목구멍; 목; 좁은 통로
Your throat is the back of your mouth and the top part of the tubes that go down into your stomach and your lungs.

choke [tʃouk] v. 숨이 막히다; 질식시키다; n. 질식
When you choke or when something chokes you, you cannot breathe properly or get enough air into your lungs.

bite [bait] n. 물기, 한 입; v. 물다, 물어뜯다
A bite of something, especially food, is the action of biting it.

jaw [dʒɔː] n. 턱, 아래턱
A person's or animal's jaws are the two bones in their head which their teeth are attached to.

just in time idiom 때마침
If you say that something happens just in time, you are emphasizing that it happens at the last possible moment.

swing [swiŋ] v. (swung-swung) 흔들다; 매달리다, 빙 돌다
If something swings or if you swing it, it moves repeatedly backwards and forwards or from side to side from a fixed point.

The Enormous Crocodile

branch [bræntʃ] n. 가지; 지점; 분파; v. 가지를 내다
The branches of a tree are the parts that grow out from its trunk and have leaves, flowers, or fruit growing on them.

roly-poly [róulipóuli] a. 땅딸막한, 통통한; n. 오뚝이 모양의 장난감; (영) 돌돌 말은 푸딩
Roly-poly people are pleasantly fat and round.

luscious [lʌ́ʃəs] a. 감미로운, 달콤한
Luscious food is juicy and very good to eat.

super-duper [sùːpərdjúːpər] a. 아주 훌륭한, 월등히 좋은
Super-duper means very excellent.

mushious 사전에 없는 저자가 합성한 단어
mushy (a. 감상적인, 연약한) + ···ious (···의 특징을 가진)

rotten [rátn] a. 썩은; 타락한, 부패한
If food, wood, or another substance is rotten, it has decayed and can no longer be used.

mash [mæʃ] vt. 찧다, 짓이기다; n. 짓이긴 것, 갈아서 빻은 것
If you mash food that is solid but soft, you crush it so that it forms a soft mass.

munch [mʌntʃ] v. 우적우적 먹다
If you munch food, you eat it by chewing it slowly, thoroughly, and rather noisily.

raspberry [rǽzbèri] n. [식물] 나무딸기
Raspberries are small, soft, red fruit that grow on bushes.

rattle [rǽtl] v. 왈각달각 소리 나다, 덜거덕 움직이다; n. 덜거덕거리는 소리
When something rattles or when you rattle it, it makes short sharp knocking sounds because it is being shaken or it keeps hitting against something hard.

penny [péni] n. 1페니 (1/100 파운드)
In Britain, a penny is one hundredth of a pound, or a coin worth this amount of money.

Build Your Vocabulary

piggy bank [pígibæŋk] n. 돼지 저금통
A piggy bank is a container in the shape of a pig, with a narrow opening in the top for putting coins in, used by children to save money.

snap [snæp] v. 덥석 물다; 홱 잡다, 짤깍 소리 내다; 날카롭게[느닷없이] 말하다; n. 툭 소리 냄
If an animal such as a dog snaps at you, it opens and shuts its jaws quickly near you, as if it were going to bite you.

feather [féðər] n. 깃털, 깃
A bird's feathers are the soft covering on its body.

shriek [ʃri:k] n. 비명; v. 새된 소리를 지르다, 비명을 지르다
A shriek is a short, very loud cry.

creep [kri:p] vi. (crept-crept) 기다, 살금살금 걷다; n. 포복
When people or animals creep somewhere, they move quietly and slowly.

grasp [græsp] v. 붙잡다, 움켜쥐다; n. 움켜잡기
If you grasp something, you take it in your hand and hold it very firmly.

paw [pɔ:] n. (동물의 갈고리 발톱이 있는) 발; v. 앞발로 차다
The paws of an animal such as a cat, dog, or bear are its feet, which have claws for gripping things and soft pads for walking on.

arrange [əréindʒ] v. 준비하다; 가지런히 하다, 배열하다
If you arrange something, you make it possible to have or to do.

peer [piər] vi. 응시하다, 자세히 보다; 희미하게 나타나다
If you peer at something, you look at it very hard.

lick [lik] vt. 핥다; (불길이) 넘실거리다; n. 전혀 (…이) 없음; 소량; 핥기
When people or animals lick something, they move their tongue across its surface.

dribble [dríbəl] v. (침 등을) 질질 흘리다; (액체가 조금씩) 똑똑 떨어지다; (공을) 드리블하다; n. (입에서 흐르는) 침; (스포츠에서의) 드리블
If a liquid dribbles somewhere, or if you dribble it, it drops down slowly or flows in a thin stream.

The Enormous Crocodile

* **tremendous** [triméndəs] a. 거대한, 대단한; 엄청난; 무서운
You use tremendous to emphasize how strong a feeling or quality is, or how large an amount is.

whoosh [hwú(:)ʃ] v. 쉭 하고 움직이다; n. (의성어) 휙[쉭]
If something whooshes somewhere, it moves there quickly or suddenly.

* **gallop** [gǽləp] v. 전속력으로 달리다, 질주하다; 전속력으로 몰다; n. 갤럽 (말 등이 전속력으로 달리기)
When a horse gallops, it runs very fast so that all four legs are off the ground at the same time.

eat up phrasal v. (…을) 다 먹다
If you eat something up, you eat all of them.

* **terrific** [tərífik] a. 굉장한, 엄청난; 무서운, 소름이 끼치는
If you describe something or someone as terrific, you are very pleased with them or very impressed by them.

* **charge** [tʃɑːrdʒ] v. 돌격하다, 돌진하다; 청구하다, 부담시키다; 채우다, 충전하다; n. 청구 금액; 책임
If you charge towards someone or something, you move quickly and aggressively towards them.

* **tumble** [tʌ́mbəl] v. 굴러 떨어지다, 넘어지다[뜨리다]; n. 추락; 폭락
If someone or something tumbles somewhere, they fall there with a rolling or bouncing movement.

skid [skid] v. 미끄러지다; n. 미끄럼, 옆으로 미끄러짐
If a vehicle skids, it slides sideways or forwards while moving, for example when you are trying to stop it suddenly on a wet road.

* **log** [lɔ(ː)g] n. 통나무; 무감각한 것, 움직임이 없는 것
A log is a piece of a thick branch or of the trunk of a tree that has been cut so that it can be used for fuel or for making things.

* **tuck** [tʌk] v. 밀어 넣다, 쑤셔 넣다; n. 접어 넣은 단
If you tuck something somewhere, you put it there so that it is safe, comfortable, or neat.

Build Your Vocabulary

seesaw [síːsɔ̀ː] n. 시소; 동요, 변동; a. 시소 같은; 동요[변동]하는; ad. 아래위[앞뒤]로 움직여; 동요하여
A seesaw is a long board which is balanced on a fixed part in the middle.

knobbly [nábli] a. 마디가 많은, 혹이 많은
Something that is knobbly has lumps on it which stick out and make the surface uneven.

jerk [dʒəːrk] n. 갑자기 잡아당김; 반사 운동; 바보, 멍청이; v. 갑자기 움직이다
A jerk is a move with a sudden movement.

yum yum [jʌmjʌm] n. 냠냠; 맛있는 것[음식]; int. 아이 맛있어!
People sometimes say 'yum yum' to show that they think something tastes or smells very good.

curse [kəːrs] vt. 저주하다, 욕설을 퍼붓다; n. 저주, 악담
If you curse, you use rude or offensive language, usually because you are angry about something.

bush [buʃ] n. 관목, 덤불, 우거진 것
A bush is a large plant which is smaller than a tree and has a lot of branches.

slide [slaid] n. 미끄럼틀; v. 미끄러지다, 미끄러지게 하다
A slide is a piece of playground equipment that has a steep slope for children to go down for fun.

dodgem [dádʒəm] n. 유원지 등에 있는 작은 전기 자동차
A dodgem car is a small electric car with a wide rubber strip all round.

cotton candy [kátnkǽndi] n. 솜사탕
Cotton candy is a large pink or white mass of sugar threads that is eaten from a stick.

merry-go-round [mérigouràund] n. 회전목마
A merry-go-round is a large circular platform at a fairground on which there are model animals or vehicles for people to sit on or in as it turns round.

The Enormous Crocodile

* **marvelous** [mάːrvələs] a. 훌륭한, 우수한; 놀라운, 믿기 어려운
If you describe someone or something as marvelous, you are emphasizing that they are very good.

* **mermaid** [máːrmèid] n. (여자) 인어(人魚)
In fairy stories and legends, a mermaid is a woman with a fish's tail instead of legs, who lives in the sea.

fearsome [fíərsəm] a. (얼굴 등이) 무시무시한; 무서워하는, 오싹한; 대단한
Fearsome is used to describe things that are frightening, for example because of their large size or extreme nature.

stick out phrasal v. 불쑥 나오다, 돌출하다
If something is sticking out from a surface or object, it extends up or away from it.

* **flock** [flɑk] vi. 무리 짓다, 모이다; n. 무리, 떼
If people flock to a particular place or event, a very large number of them go there, usually because it is pleasant or interesting.

swish [swiʃ] n. 휙 소리; 일격; v. 휘두르다, 휙 소리내다
If something swishes or if you swish it, it moves quickly through the air, making a soft sound.

* **bunch** [bʌntʃ] n. 다량; 다발, 송이; 떼, 한패
A bunch of things is a number of things, especially a large number.

* **chest** [tʃest] ① n. 가슴; 흉곽 ② n. 상자, 궤
Your chest is the top part of the front of your body where your ribs, lungs, and heart are.

* **twist** [twist] v. 돌리다, 꼬다, 비틀다; n. 뒤틀림, 엉킴, 변화
If you twist something, you turn it to make a spiral shape.

as quiet as a mouse idiom 쥐 죽은 듯이 조용한
If you describe something as quiet as a mouse, it makes very little noise.

swizzle [swízəl] v. 휘젓다; 술을 벌컥벌컥 마시다; n. 혼합주, 칵테일
If you swizzle something, you mix or stir it.

Build Your Vocabulary

- **bellow** [bélou] vi. 고함지르다; 큰 소리로 울다
  If someone bellows, they shout angrily in a loud, deep voice.

- **trot** [trɑt] v. 빠른 걸음으로 가다; 총총걸음 치다; n. 빠른 걸음
  If you trot somewhere, you move fairly fast at a speed between walking and running, taking small quick step.

- **spot** [spɑt] n. 장소, 지점; 반점, 얼룩; vt. 발견하다, 분별하다
  You can refer to a particular place as a spot.

- **trunk** [trʌŋk] n. 코끼리 코; (나무의) 줄기; 여행 가방
  An elephant's trunk is its very long nose that it uses to lift food and water to its mouth.

- **hoist** [hɔist] vt. 올리다, 높이 달다, 끌어올리다; n. 감아올리기; 감아올리는 기계
  If you hoist something heavy somewhere, you lift it or pull it up there.

- **yell** [jel] v. 소리치다, 고함치다; n. 고함소리, 부르짖음
  If you yell, you shout loudly, usually because you are excited, angry, or in pain.

- **dangle** [dǽŋɡəl] v. (달랑달랑) 매달(리)다; n. 매달린 것
  If something dangles from somewhere or if you dangle it somewhere, it hangs or swings loosely.

- **blurry** [blə́:ri] a. 흐릿한; 더러워진
  A blurry shape is one that has an unclear outline.

- **whizz** [hwiz] v. 씽[윙] 소리를 내며 움직이다[날다]
  If something whizzes somewhere, it moves there very fast.

- **headfirst** [hédfə́:rst] ad. 거꾸로, 곤두박질로; 황급히; 무턱대고
  If you move headfirst in a particular direction, your head is the part of your body that is furthest forward as you are moving.

- **planet** [plǽnət] n. 행성
  A planet is a large, round object in space that moves around a star.

- **sizzle** [sízəl] v. (튀김이나 고기 구울 때) 지글지글하다
  If something such as hot oil or fat sizzles, it makes hissing sounds.

The Enormous Crocodile

The Giraffe and the Pelly and Me

Comprehension Quiz

1. Why didn't the boy go inside of The Grubber?

   A. He was too scared.

   B. The door was always locked.

   C. People lived inside of the shop.

   D. His mother would be angry.

2. Long ago, The Grubber was a _____.

   A. furniture store

   B. candy store

   C. pet store

   D. paint store

3. The boy dreamed about _____.

   A. owning a candy store

   B. washing windows

   C. having fun pets

   D. having a new house

4. What did the boy see in the morning?

   A. He saw a very big window.

   B. He saw new paint on the walls.

   C. He saw a very tall door.

   D. He saw new furniture inside of the store.

The Giraffe and the Pelly and Me

5. Put the events in order: (– – – –)

A. The boy called out, "Is anybody home?"

B. The boy saw FOR SAIL was on The Grubber's window.

C. The boy read the writing on the window.

D. Someone threw things out of The Grubber's window.

E. Someone wrote SOLED on the Grubber's window.

Comprehension Quiz

6. Put the events in order: (–   –   –   –   )

  A. The boy saw the Monkey.

  B. The boy climbed into the Pelican's beak.

  C. The boy saw the Pelican.

  D. The boy saw the Giraffe.

  E. The Pelican sang a song.

7. The _____ danced very well.

  A. Boy

  B. Monkey

  C. Pelican

  D. Giraffe

8. What work did the Pelican, Giraffe, and Monkey do?

  A. They sang songs for money.

  B. They washed windows.

  C. They sold candy.

  D. They painted houses.

9. Why did the top half of the Pelican's beak slide backward?

  A. He could eat a lot of fish.

  B. He could carry the Monkey.

  C. He could carry paint.

  D. He could hold window cleaning water.

The Giraffe and the Pelly and Me

10. Who needed expensive food?

A. The boy

B. The Giraffe

C. The Pelican

D. The Monkey

Comprehension Quiz

11. The Duke of Hampshire is _____.

   A. the richest man in England

   B. the meanest man in England

   C. the richest man in the world

   D. the smartest man in Hampshire

12. The Hampshire house had _____ windows.

   A. 100

   B. 450

   C. 677

   D. 1002

13. The Duke thought that _____.

   A. the Giraffe was eating his fruit

   B. the Pelican was stealing his fruit

   C. the Giraffe was eating leaves

   D. Billy was climbing the tree

14. Put the events in order: (–   –   –   –   )

   A. The Chauffeur read the message.

   B. Billy and the animals saw the Hampshire House.

   C. The Monkey jumped on the Giraffe's back.

   D. Billy picked the fruit from the tree.

   E. Billy and the animals heard a man yelling.

The Giraffe and the Pelly and Me

15. Match the character with the quotation:

1. The Pelican   A. "Just look at those windows! They'll keep us going for ever!"

2. Billy   B. "Pick them quickly and put them in my beak!"

3. The Monkey   C. "I can't reach them, Your Grace. The ladder isn't long enough!"

4. The Gardener   D. "I want those big black ones at the top of the tree!"

5. The Duke   E. "It's called the Hampshire House. It's just over the hill. I'll show you the way."

Comprehension Quiz

16. Complete the sentences:

1. The Pelican···   A. is the cleaner.
2. Billy···   B. is the business manager.
3. The Monkey···   C. wants his windows cleaned.
4. The Giraffe···   D. is the bucket.
5. The Duke···   E. is the ladder.

17. The Duke wants Billy and the animals to _____ next autumn.

A. clean his cars
B. pick flowers
C. pick apples
D. plant seeds

18. Put the events in order: (–   –   –   –   )

A. The Pelican filled his beak with water.
B. The Pelican perched on a window-sill.
C. The Monkey cleaned a window.
D. The Monkey turned on the garden tap.
E. The Monkey climbed up the Giraffe's neck onto the Giraffe's head.

19. Billy said, "If you wish to be friends with a Giraffe, _____."

   A. never say anything bad about its neck
   B. never talk to it when it's working
   C. never say anything bad about its spots
   D. never yell at it

20. What is special about the Giraffe?

   A. Its legs can grow longer.
   B. Its horns can grow bigger.
   C. Its neck can grow longer.
   D. It can fly.

Comprehension Quiz

21. The animals stopped moving because _____.

　A. the Duke yelled at the Giraffe

　B. the animals saw a dirty window

　C. they heard the Duchess singing

　D. they saw a thief

22. Why was there a BANG inside of the Pelican's beak?

　A. The thief punched the Pelican's beak.

　B. The Pelican shook his head.

　C. The thief shot his gun.

　D. The thief kicked the Pelican's beak.

23. What did the Pelican do when the thief was in his beak?

　A. He shook his head.

　B. He flew upside down.

　C. He tried to swallow the thief.

　D. He hit the thief.

The Giraffe and the Pelly and Me

24. The thief stole _____.

   A. the Duchess's wedding ring

   B. the Duke's money

   C. the Duchess's diamonds

   D. the Duke's paintings

25. How did the thief get into the Duchess's room?

   A. He climbed the drain pipe.

   B. He broke the window.

   C. He unlocked the door.

   D. He dug a hole in the roof.

Comprehension Quiz

26. What was wrong with the Pelican?

   A. He couldn't move his beak.

   B. The thief hurt his wing.

   C. There was a hole in his beak.

   D. He couldn't fly.

27. Complete the sentences:

   1. The Pelican ate⋯   A. flowers from the tinkle-tinkle trees.

   2. The Giraffe ate⋯   B. walnuts from big nut trees.

   3. The Monkey ate⋯   C. salmon from the river.

The Giraffe and the Pelly and Me

28. Why did the Duke reward the animals?

    A. They were very kind animals.

    B. They washed all of the windows.

    C. They saved the Duchess's diamonds.

    D. The Duchess wanted to keep the animals as pets.

29. Match the character with the quotation:

    1. The Pelican   A. "Oh my naked neck! I cannot believe what I am seeing!"

    2. The Duke   B. "A pleasure, Your Grace! Would you like a ride now?"

    3. The Monkey   C. "You don't really mean walnuts? You're pulling my leg."

    4. The Giraffe   D. "Those diamonds were worth millions! Millions and millions! and you have saved them!"

30. What will the animals do for the Duke?

    A. They will paint his house and clean his windows.

    B. They will pick his fruit and make his tea.

    C. They will cook his food and clean his house.

    D. They will clean his windows and pick his fruit.

Comprehension Quiz

31. What did Billy wish for?

   A. He wished for a big bag of candy.

   B. He wished to live at the Hampshire House.

   C. He wished to open The Grubber shop.

   D. He wished to travel to different countries.

32. Why was it easy to buy The Grubber?

   A. The building was cheap.

   B. The animals gave the Duke the building.

   C. The Grubber was very small.

   D. The Duke was very rich and he bought the building.

33. Put the events in order: (–   –   –   –   )

   A. The candy was delivered to the store.

   B. Builders and carpenters rebuilt the inside of the building.

   C. Customers got free candy.

   D. The boy gave the Duke and the animals some candy.

   E. The animals left the shop because they had to clean windows.

34. Complete the sentences:

   1. The Giraffe ate···   A. Pishlets.

   2. The Duke ate···   B. Devil's Drenchers.

   3. The Pelican ate···   C. Scarlet Scorchdroppers.

   4. The Monkey ate···   D. Glumptious Globgobblers.

The Giraffe and the Pelly and Me

35. Match the Candy with its description:

1. Giant Wangdoodles

2. Electric Fizzcocklers

3. Willy Wonka's Rainbow Drops

4. Mint Jujubes

A. Let a person spit seven different colors.

B. Have a strawberry inside their chocolate crust.

C. Make a person's teeth green.

D. Make a person's hair stand up.

Build Your Vocabulary

queer [kwiər] a. 별난, 기묘한, 이상한
Something that is queer is strange.

long [lɔːŋ] ① vi. 간절히 바라다, 동경하다 ② a. 긴, 오랜
If you long to do something, you want it very much, especially when it seems unlikely to happen soon.

peer [piər] vi. 응시하다, 자세히 보다; 희미하게 나타나다
If you peer at something, you look at it very hard.

fade [feid] vi. 바래다, 시들다, 희미해지다 (faded a. 빛깔이 바랜)
When a colored object fades or when the light fades it, it gradually becomes paler.

grubber [grʌ́bər] n. (= moneygrubber) 수전노; 나무 그루터기[뿌리]를 파내는 사람
A grubber is someone who scavenges in drains for a living.

sweet-shop [swíːtʃɑ̀p] n. (영) 과자점
A sweet-shop is a small shop that sells sweets and cigarettes, and sometimes newspapers and magazines.

FOR SAIL FOR SALE(팔려고 내놓은)을 잘못 표기한 것

scrape [skreip] v. 긁어내다, 벗겨내다[떼다]; 문지르다; n. 문지름, 긁음
If you scrape something from a surface, you remove it, especially by pulling a sharp object over the surface.

SOLED SOLD(판매됨)을 잘못 표기한 것

sherbet [ʃə́ːrbit] n. 셔벗 (과즙 아이스크림)
Sherbet is like ice cream but made with fruit juice, sugar, and water.

fudge [fʌdʒ] n. (초콜릿·버터·밀크·설탕 따위로 만든) 연한 캔디
Fudge is a soft brown sweet that is made from butter, cream, and sugar.

toffee [tɔ́ːfi] n. (= taffy) 태피 (설탕, 버터 따위로 만든 과자)
Toffee is a sticky sweet that you chew.

glorious [glɔ́ːriəs] a. 찬란한, 훌륭한, 영광스러운
Something that is glorious is very beautiful and impressive.

The Giraffe and the Pelly and Me

gaze [geiz] vi. 응시하다, 지켜보다; n. 응시, 주시
If you gaze at someone or something, you look steadily at them for a long time.

enormous [inɔ́ːrməs] a. 엄청난, 거대한, 막대한
Something that is enormous is extremely large in size or amount.

bathtub [bǽθtʌ̀b] n. 욕조
A bathtub is a long, usually rectangular container which you fill with water and sit in to wash your body.

sail [seil] v. 뻗어나가다; 항해하다, 출항하다
If a person or thing sails somewhere, they move there quickly.

crash [kræʃ] vt. 충돌하다, 추락하다, 와르르 무너지다; n. 충돌, 추락
If something crashes somewhere, it moves and hits something else violently, making a loud noise.

porcelain [pɔ́ːrsəlin] a. 자기 같은, 자기로 만든; 깨지기 쉬운; n. 자기, 자기 제품
Porcelain is a hard, shiny substance made by heating clay which is used to make delicate cups, plates, and ornaments.

lavatory [lǽvətɔ̀ːri] n. 변기; 세면장, 화장실
A lavatory is a large bowl with a seat, or a platform with a hole, which is connected to a water system.

splinter [splíntər] v. 쪼개지다, 산산조각이 되다; n. 부서진 조각
If something splinters or is splintered, it breaks into thin, sharp pieces.

canary [kənɛ́əri] n. 카나리아
Canaries are small yellow birds which sing beautifully and are often kept as pets.

cage [keidʒ] n. 새장, 우리; vt. 새장[우리]에 넣다
A cage is a structure of wire or metal bars in which birds or animals are kept.

four-poster bed n. 사주식 침대 (4개의 기둥과 커튼으로 장식된 큰 침대)
A four-poster bed is a large old-fashioned bed that has a tall post at each corner and curtains that can be drawn around it.

Build Your Vocabulary

rocking horse n. 장난감 흔들 목마
A rocking horse is a toy horse which a child can sit on and which can be made to rock backwards and forwards.

sewing-machine n. 재봉틀
A sewing-machine is a machine that you use for sewing.

* **rip** [rip] v. 찢다, 벗겨내다; 돌진하다; n. 찢어진 틈; 잡아 찢음
When something rips or when you rip it, you tear it forcefully with your hands or with a tool such as a knife.

* **staircase** [stéərkèis] n. 계단, 층계
A staircase is a set of stairs inside a building.

banister [bǽnistər] n. 계단의 난간
A banister is a rail supported by posts and fixed along the side of a staircase.

floorboard [flɔ́:rbɔ̀:rd] n. 바닥 널, 바닥
Floorboards are the long pieces of wood that a wooden floor is made up of.

* **whistle** [hwísəl] v. 팽 하고 날아가다; 휘파람 불다; n. 휘파람; 호각
If something such as the wind or a bullet whistles somewhere, it moves there, making a loud, high sound.

you can bet your life idiom 틀림없이 …이다, 당연하다
목숨을 걸 수 있을 정도로 확신한다는 뜻이다.

* **notice** [nóutis] vt. 알아차리다, 주의하다; n. 주의, 주목
If you notice something or someone, you become aware of them.

brand-new [brǽndnjù:] a. 아주 새로운, 신상품의
A brand-new object is completely new.

* **ridiculous** [ridíkjələs] a. 터무니없는; 웃기는, 우스꽝스러운
If you say that something or someone is ridiculous, you mean that they are very foolish.

* **tremendous** [triméndəs] a. 거대한, 대단한; 엄청난, 무서운
You use tremendous to emphasize how strong a feeling or quality is, or how large an amount is.

The Giraffe and the Pelly and Me

figure out phrasal v. …을 생각해내다, 발견하다
If you figure out a solution to a problem or the reason for something, you succeed in solving it or understanding it.

fling [fliŋ] vt. (flung–flung) (문 등을) 왈칵 열다; 내던지다, 던지다
If you fling something somewhere, you throw it there using a lot of force.

gigantic [dʒaigǽntik] a. 거대한, 막대한
If you describe something as gigantic, you are emphasizing that it is extremely large in size, amount, or degree.

hop [hɑp] v. 깡충 뛰다, 뛰어 오르다; n. 깡충깡충 뜀
If you hop, you move along by jumping.

perch [pəːrtʃ] v. (높은 곳에) 앉(히)다, 놓다
If you perch on something, you sit down lightly on the very edge or tip of it.

window-sill n. 창턱, 창 아래틀
A window-sill is a shelf along the bottom of a window, either inside or outside a building.

beak [biːk] n. 새의 부리
A bird's beak is the hard curved or pointed part of its mouth.

basin [béisən] n. 물동이, 대야, 세면기
A basin is a large or deep bowl that you use for holding liquids.

pelican [pélikən] n. [조류] 펠리컨
A pelican is a type of large water bird which catches fish and keeps them in the bottom part of its beak which is shaped like a large bag.

fishmonger [fíʃmʌŋgər] n. (영) 생선 장수, 생선 가게
A fishmonger is a shopkeeper who sells fish.

on earth idiom [의문사를 강조하여] 도대체, 어떻게
You use 'on earth' with questions, in order to express your surprise or anger.

fish-cake [fíʃkeik] n. 어묵, 어육 완자
A fish cake is a mixture of fish and potato that is made into a flat round shape, covered in breadcrumbs, and fried.

Build Your Vocabulary

fish-finger [fíʃfíŋgər] n. 가늘고 긴 생선 토막 튀김
Fish-fingers are small long pieces of fish, covered in breadcrumbs.

* **baffle** [bǽfəl] v. 당황하게 하다; 헛수고 하다
If something baffles you, you cannot understand it or explain it.

jiggle [dʒígəl] v. 가볍게 흔들다, 가볍게 당기다 (jiggly a. 흔들리는, 불안정한)
If you jiggle something, you move it quickly up and down or from side to side.

furry [fə́:ri] a. 털로 덮인, 부드러운 털의
If you describe something as furry, you mean that it has a soft rough texture like fur.

* **clap** [klæp] v. 박수를[손뼉을] 치다; 가볍게 치다[두드리다]
When you clap, you hit your hands together to show appreciation or attract attention.

* **polish** [páliʃ] v. 닦다, 윤내다; n. 광택; 세련
If you polish something, you rub it with a cloth to make it shine.

* **brass** [bræs] n. 놋쇠, 황동
Brass is a yellow-colored metal made from copper and zinc.

* **sparkle** [spá:rkəl] v. 반짝이다, 불꽃을 튀기다; n. 불꽃, 광채
If something sparkles, it is clear and bright and shines with a lot of very small points of light.

* **fabulous** [fǽbjələs] a. 굉장한, 멋진; 믿어지지 않는; 전설적인
If you describe something as fabulous, you are emphasizing that you like it a lot or think that it is very good.

* **crew** [kru:] n. 동료, 패거리; 승무원, 선원
A crew is a group of people with special technical skills who work together on a task or project.

* **glow** [glou] v. 빛을 내다; n. 빛, 밝음
If something glows, it produces a dull, steady light.

The Giraffe and the Pelly and Me

ladder [lǽdər] n. 사다리
A ladder is a piece of equipment used for climbing up something or down from something.

enthral [enθrɔ́:l] vt. …의 마음을 사로잡다, 매혹시키다, 홀리게 하다
If you are enthralled by something, you enjoy it and give it your complete attention and interest.

spread [spred] v. 펴다, 펼치다; 뿌리다; n. 퍼짐, 폭, 넓이
If you spread your arms, hands, fingers, or legs, you stretch them out until they are far apart.

swallow [swάlou] v. (꿀꺽) 삼키다, 들이켜다; 싸다, 덮다; n. 삼킴, 마심
If you swallow something, you cause it to go from your mouth down into your stomach.

swear [swɛər] v. 맹세하다, 단언하다; 욕을 하다; n. 맹세, 선서
If you swear to do something, you promise in a serious way that you will do it.

bend [bend] v. 구부러지다, 휘다; 구부리다, 돌리다; n. 커브, 굽음
When you bend a part of your body such as your arm or leg, or when it bends, you change its position so that it is no longer straight.

sensible [sénsəbəl] a. 상식적인, 분별 있는; 느낄 수 있는
Sensible actions or decisions are good because they are based on reasons rather than emotions.

tape-measure n. (천 또는 금속으로 만든) 줄자; v. 줄자로 재다
A tape measure is a strip of metal, plastic, or cloth which has numbers marked on it and is used for measuring.

precise [prisáis] a. 정확한, 정밀한; 명확한 (precisely ad. 정밀하게, 정확히)
You use precise to emphasize that you are referring to an exact thing, rather than something vague.

count [kaunt] v. 중요하다; 세다, 셈에 넣다; n. 계산
If something or someone counts for something or counts, they are important or valuable.

Build Your Vocabulary

lad [læd] n. 젊은이, 청년, 소년
A lad is a young man or boy.

flown [floun] v. fly(날다)의 과거분사 (fly–flew–flown)
Flown is the past participle of fly.

patent [pǽtənt] v. 특허를 받다; n. 특허 (patented a. 독특한, 특징적인)
If you patent something, you obtain an official right to be the only person or company allowed to make or sell it.

tweak [twi:k] n. 비틀기, 꼬집음; vt. 비틀다, 꼬집다
A tweak is a squeeze with fingers.

blink [bliŋk] n. (눈을) 깜박거림; v. 눈을 깜박거리다; (등불·별 등이) 깜박이다
A blink is a reflex that closes and opens the eyes rapidly.

swoosh [swuʃ] n. 휙[쉭] 소리; v. 휙[쉭] 소리를 내다
Swoosh is the noise produced by the sudden rush.

perch [pəːrtʃ] n. (새의) 횃대; 높은[안전한] 자리; v. (높은 곳에) 놓다, 앉히다
You can refer to a high place where someone is sitting as their perch.

penny [péni] n. 1페니 (1/100 파운드)
If you say that something or someone is worth every penny, you mean that they are worth all the money that is spent on them.

starve [sta:rv] v. 굶주리다, 굶어죽다; 갈망하다
If people starve, they suffer greatly from lack of food which sometimes leads to their death.

famish [fǽmiʃ] vt. 굶주리게 하다
If you are famished, you are very hungry.

perish [périʃ] v. (추위·기아 등으로) 죽(게 하)다; 멸망하다, 소멸하다
If people or animals perish, they die as a result of very harsh conditions or as the result of an accident.

tinkle [tíŋkəl] v. 딸랑딸랑 울리다; n. 딸랑딸랑, 따르릉
If something tinkles, it makes a clear, high-pitched, ringing noise, especially as small parts of it strike a surface.

The Giraffe and the Pelly and Me

* **stale** [steil] a. (음식 따위가) 상한, 신선하지 않은
  Stale food is no longer fresh or good to eat.

* **sardine** [sɑːrdíːn] n. [어류] 정어리
  Sardines are a kind of small sea fish, often eaten as food.

* **bucket** [bʌ́kit] n. 양동이, 버킷
  A bucket is a round metal or plastic container with a handle attached to its sides.

* **rotten** [rátn] a. 썩은; 타락한, 부패한
  If food, wood, or another substance is rotten, it has decayed and can no longer be used.

  cod [kɑd] n. [어류] 대구
  Cod are a type of large edible fish.

  bod [bɑd] n. (영·속어) 사람, 놈, 녀석
  A bod is a person.

* **salmon** [sǽmən] n. [어류] 연어
  A salmon is a large silver-colored fish.

* **walnut** [wɔ́ːlnʌ̀t] n. [식물] 호두(열매); 호두나무
  Walnuts are edible nuts which have a wrinkled shape and a hard round shell that is light brown in color.

  scrumptious [skrʌ́mpʃəs] a. (구어) 굉장히 맛있는; 굉장한, 훌륭한
  If you describe food as scrumptious, you mean that it tastes extremely good.

  galumptious 사전에 없는 저자가 만든 단어로 매우 좋다는 의미

* **flavor** [fléivər] vt. 풍미를 더하다; n. 풍미, 맛; 멋 (flavory a. 풍미가 풍부한, 향기로운)
  If you flavor food or drink, you add something to it to give it a particular taste.

  savory [séivəri] a. 맛좋은, 향긋한; 즐거운, 기분 좋은
  Savory food has a salty or spicy flavor rather than a sweet one.

Build Your Vocabulary

wobbly [wábəli] a. 흔들거리는, 동요하는, 불안정한; 줏대 없는
Something that is wobbly moves unsteadily from side to side.

Rolls-Royce n. 롤스로이스 (영국의 고급 자동차)

pull up phrasal v. 차를 세우다, (말·차 등이) 서다
When a vehicle or driver pulls up, the vehicle slows down and stops.

★ **chauffeur** [ʃóufər] n. (자가용차의) 운전사
The chauffeur of a rich or important person is the man or woman who is employed to look after their car and drive them around in it.

Good heavens idiom (놀람의 소리) 큰일이군! 어머나! 아뿔싸!
People sometimes say 'Good heavens' to express surprise, especially when they are annoyed.

‡ **duke** [dju:k] n. (귀족) 공작
A duke is a man with a very high social rank.

‡ **decent** [dí:sənt] a. 적당한; (사회 기준에) 맞는; 점잖은
Decent is used to describe something which is considered to be of an acceptable standard or quality.

★ **filthy** [fílθi] a. 불결한, 더러운
Something that is filthy is very dirty indeed.

‡ **awe** [ɔ:] n. 경외, 외경심; vt. 경외하게 하다; 위압하여 …시키다
Awe is the feeling of respect and amazement that you have when you are faced with something wonderful and often rather frightening.

‡ **stoop** [stu:p] v. 웅크리다, 상체를 굽히다[구부리다]
If you stoop, you bend your body forwards and downwards.

flower-bed [fláuərbéd] n. 화단
flower (n. 꽃, 화초) + bed (n. 장소, 화단)

‡ **bush** [buʃ] n. 관목, 덤불, 우거진 것
A bush is a large plant which is smaller than a tree and has a lot of branches.

The Giraffe and the Pelly and Me

oldish [óuldiʃ] a. 늙수그레한, 예스러운
Oldish means fairly old.

immense [iméns] a. 막대한, 무한한, 광대한
If you describe something as immense, you mean that it is extremely large or great.

moustache [mʌ́stæʃ] n. (= mustache) (영) 코밑수염
A man's moustache is the hair that grows on his upper lip.

damnation [dæmnéiʃən] int. 제기랄, 젠장! (= damn); n. 저주, 욕설, 악평
Some people say 'damnation' to express anger or impatience.

swish [swiʃ] n. 휙 소리; v. 휙 소리 내다, 휘두르다; 튀기다
Swish is a soft sound made by movement of air.

swoop [swu:p] n. 급강하; v. 내리 덮치다, 급강하하다
Swoop is the act of suddenly plunging downward.

damnable [dǽmnəbəl] a. 몹시 싫은, 지긋지긋한
You use damnable to emphasize that you dislike or disapprove of something a great deal.

steal [sti:l] v. 훔치다
If you steal something from someone, you take it away from them without their permission and without intending to return it.

idiot [ídiət] n. 얼간이, 바보
If you call someone an idiot, you are showing that you think they are very stupid or have done something very stupid.

thieving [θí:viŋ] a. 도둑질의
Thieving means involved in stealing things or intending to steal something.

furious [fjúəriəs] a. 격노한; 맹렬한, 왕성한
Someone who is furious is extremely angry.

Build Your Vocabulary

- **prance** [præns] vi. 여기저기 뛰어 다니다, 껑충거리며 나아가다; n. (말의) 날뛰기; 활보
  If someone prances around, they walk or move around with exaggerated movements, usually because they want people to look at them and admire them.

- **lean** [li:n] v. 상체를 굽히다, 기울(이)다; 기대다, 의지하다
  When you lean in a particular direction, you bend your body in that direction.

- **handful** [hǽndfùl] n. 한 움큼, 손에 가득, 한 줌
  A handful of something is the amount of it that you can hold in your hand.

- **stagger** [stǽgər] v. 비틀거리다; 흔들리게 하다; 주저하다; n. 비틀거림
  If you stagger, you walk very unsteadily, for example because you are ill or drunk.

- **reel** [ri:l] ① v. 비틀거리다; (마음이) 어지럽다; n. 현기증 ② n. 릴, 실패; v. (실을 물레 등에) 감다
  If you are reeling from a shock, you are feeling extremely surprised or upset because of it.

- **socket** [sákit] n. 꽂는[끼우는] 구멍; vt. 소켓에 끼우다
  A socket is a device on a piece of electrical equipment into which you can put a bulb or plug.

- **Great Scott** idiom 저런, 아이고, 아 놀랐다!
  'Great Scott' is an exclamation of surprise or amazement.

- **gasp** [gæsp] v. (놀람 따위로) 숨이 막히다, 헐떡거리다; n. 헐떡거림
  When you gasp, you take a short quick breath through your mouth, especially when you are surprised, shocked, or in pain.

- **emerge** [imə́:rdʒ] vi. 나오다, 나타나다
  To emerge means to come out from an enclosed or dark space.

- **fit** [fit] ① n. 발작, 경련 ② v. 끼우다, 맞게 하다, 적합하다; a. 적합한
  If someone has a fit, they suddenly lose consciousness and their body makes uncontrollable movements.

- **bellow** [bélou] v. 큰 소리로 울다; 고함지르다; n. 울부짖는 소리; 고함소리
  If someone bellows, they shout angrily in a loud, deep voice.

The Giraffe and the Pelly and Me

dotty [dɑ́ti] a. 머리가 돈; 점이 있는; 점 같은
If you say that someone is dotty, you mean that they are slightly mad or likely to do strange things.

dawn [dɔːn] vi. (일이) 점점 분명해지다; (생각이) 떠오르다; 날이 새다, 밝아지다;
n. 새벽, 동틀 녘
If a fact or idea dawns on you, you realize it.

spit [spit] v. (spat-spat) (침 등을) 뱉다; 내뱉듯이 말하다; n. 침
If you spit liquid or food somewhere, you force a small amount of it out of your mouth.

mutter [mʌ́tər] v. 중얼거리다, 불평하다; n. 중얼거림, 불평
If you mutter, you speak very quietly so that you cannot easily be heard, often because you are complaining about something.

gang [gæŋ] n. 패거리, 한 떼, 일단; v. 일단이 되다, 집단으로 행동하다
A gang is a group of people who go around together and often deliberately cause trouble.

spring into action idiom 즉각 행동을 개시하다
If you spring into action, you suddenly start working or doing something.

tap [tæp] ① n. 주둥이, (수도 등의) 꼭지 ② v. 가볍게 두드리다; n. 가볍게 두드리기
A tap is a device that controls the flow of a liquid or gas from a pipe or container.

springy [spríŋi] a. 용수철 같은; 탄력[탄성]이 있는; 경쾌한, 걸음이 빠른
If something is springy, it returns quickly to its original shape after you press it.

leap [liːp] v. 껑충 뛰다; 뛰어넘다; n. 뜀, 도약
If you leap, you jump high in the air or jump a long distance.

scramble [skrǽmbəl] v. 기어오르다; 서로 (다투어) 빼앗다; 뒤섞다; n. 기어오르기
If you scramble over rocks or up a hill, you move quickly over them or up it using your hands to help you.

possession [pəzéʃən] n. 소유; 입수; 점거, 점령
If you are in possession of something, you have it, because you have obtained it or because it belongs to you.

Build Your Vocabulary

- **snap** [snæp] v. 날카롭게[느닷없이] 말하다; 홱 잡다, 짤깍 소리 내다; n. 툭 소리 냄
  If someone snaps at you, they speak to you in a sharp, unfriendly way.

- **superior** [səpíəriər] a. 잘난 체하는; 뛰어난, 보다 나은; 우수한, 고급의
  If you describe someone as superior, you disapprove of them because they behave as if they are better, more important, or more intelligent than other people.

- **venture** [véntʃər] v. 위험을 무릅쓰고 하다; n. 모험
  If you venture to do something that requires courage or is risky, you do it.

- **astonish** [əstániʃ] vt. 깜짝 놀라게 하다 (astonishing a. 정말 놀라운, 믿기 힘든)
  If something or someone astonishes you, they surprise you very much.

- **remarkable** [rimá:rkəbəl] a. 비범한, 뛰어난; 주목할 만한
  Someone or something that is remarkable is unusual or special in a way that makes people notice them and be surprised or impressed.

- **incredible** [inkrédəbəl] a. 놀라운, 훌륭한, 믿어지지 않는
  If you describe something or someone as incredible, you like them very much or are impressed by them, because they are extremely or unusually good.

- **stop dead** idiom (사람·기계가) 딱[갑자기] 멈추다
  If you say something is stop dead, it stops moving or becomes immobilized.

- **in one's tracks** idiom 그 자리에서; 당장에, 즉각, 갑자기
  In someone's tracks means just where he or she is at the moment.

- **freeze** [fri:z] v. 얼(게 하)다, 얼어붙(게 하)다; n. 결빙
  If someone who is moving freezes, they suddenly stop and become completely still and quiet.

- **tiptoe** [típtòu] vi. 발끝으로 걷다; 발돋움하다; n. 발끝
  If you tiptoe somewhere, you walk there very quietly without putting your heels on the floor when you walk.

The Giraffe and the Pelly and Me

gingerly [dʒíndʒərli] ad. 지극히 조심스럽게, 주의 깊게
If you do something gingerly, you do it in a careful manner, usually because you expect it to be dangerous, unpleasant, or painful.

drawer [drɔ́:ər] n. 서랍
A drawer is part of a desk, chest, or other piece of furniture that is shaped like a box and is designed for putting things in.

pistol [pístl] n. 권총, 피스톨
A pistol is a small gun which is held in and fired from one hand.

by Gad idiom 저런; 하느님께 맹세코
People use 'by Gad' to emphasize how determined or surprised they are.

duchess [dʌ́tʃis] n. 공작부인, 여 공작
A duchess is a woman who has the same rank as a duke, or who is a duke's wife or widow.

summon [sʌ́mən] vt. 소환하다, 호출하다; (용기 등을) 내다, 불러일으키다
If you summon someone, you order them to come to you.

cannon [kǽnən] n. 대포; v. 대포를 쏘다, (…에) 세게 충돌하다
An old type of large heavy gun, usually on wheels, that fires solid metal or stone balls.

charge [tʃɑ:rdʒ] v. 돌격하다, 돌진하다; 청구하다; 부담시키다; 채우다, 충전하다; n. 청구 금액; 책임
If you charge towards someone or something, you move quickly and aggressively towards them.

brigade [brigéid] n. (군대식 편성의) 대(隊), 조(組)
A brigade is one of the groups which an army is divided into.

upside-down [ʌ́psaiddáun] ad. 거꾸로, 뒤집혀
If something has been moved upside-down, it has been turned round so that the part that is usually lowest is above the part that is usually highest.

tip [tip] ① v. 기울이다; 뒤집어엎다; n. 기울임 ② n. 끝, 첨단 ③ n. 팁, 사례금; v. 사례금을 주다
If you tip something somewhere, you pour it there.

Build Your Vocabulary

- **marvellous** [má:rvələs] a. 훌륭한, 우수한; 놀라운, 믿기 어려운
  If you describe someone or something as marvellous, you are emphasizing that they are very good.

- **lawn** [lɔ:n] n. 잔디, 잔디밭
  A lawn is an area of grass that is kept cut short and is usually part of someone's garden or backyard, or part of a park.

  sledgehammer [slédʒhæ̀mər] n. (두 손으로 휘두르는 대장간의) 큰 쇠망치[해머]
  A sledgehammer is a large, heavy hammer with a long handle, used for breaking up rocks and concrete.

- **burglar** [bə́:rglər] n. (주거 침입) 강도
  A burglar is a thief who enters a house or other building by force.

  walking-stick [wɔ́:kiŋstik] n. 지팡이
  A walking-stick is a long wooden stick which a person can lean on while walking.

- **hollow** [hálou] n. 구멍; 움푹한 곳; a. 속이 빈; 오목한; v. 속이 비다
  A hollow is a hole inside a tree.

- **sword** [sɔ:rd] n. 검(劍), 칼
  A sword is a weapon with a handle and a long sharp blade.

- **flourish** [flə́:riʃ] v. 팔[무기 등]을 휘두르다; 과장된 몸짓을 하다; 번창하다; n. 화려한[과장된] 몸짓
  If you flourish an object, you wave it about in a way that makes people notice it.

  fencer [fénsər] n. 검객, 검술가
  A fencer is person who takes part in the sport of fencing.

  run through phrasal v. (바늘·칼 등을) …에 찌르다; …을 대충 훑어보다
  If you run through something, you transfix it with a sword or other weapon.

  bounder [báundər] n. 천한 사람, 버릇없는 사람
  If you call a man a bounder, you mean he behaves in an unkind, deceitful, or selfish way.

The Giraffe and the Pelly and Me

pat [pæt] n. (버터 등의) 작은 덩어리; 톡톡[가볍게] 침[두드림]; v. 가볍게 치다, 토닥거리다
A pat of butter or something else that is soft is a small lump of it.

gizzard [gízərd] n. (구어·익살) (사람의) 내장, 위장; (조류의) 모래주머니
The gizzard is the part of the stomach that grinds up food.

foxhound [fákshàund] n. 여우 사냥개
A foxhound is a type of dog that is trained to hunt foxes.

arm [ɑːrm] ① vt. 무장시키다; n. 무기 ② n. 팔; (의자의) 팔걸이
If you arm someone with a weapon, you provide them with a weapon.

machine-gun [məʃíːngʌ̀n] n. 기관총
A machine-gun is a gun which fires a lot of bullets one after the other very quickly.

massive [mǽsiv] a. 크고 무거운, 육중한, 굳센, 강력한
Something that is massive is very large in size, quantity, or extent.

bristle [brísəl] v. 곤두세우다; 벌컥 화내다; n. 센털, 강모
If the hair on a person's or animal's body bristles, it rises away from their skin because they are cold, frightened, or angry.

brushwood [brʌ́ʃwùd] n. 잘라 낸 곁가지; 관목숲[덤불]
Brushwood consists of small pieces of wood that have broken off trees and bushes.

blighter [bláitər] n. 녀석; 지독한 놈, 악당
You can use blighter as an informal way of referring to someone.

ear-splitting [íərsplìtiŋ] a. 귀청이 찢어질 듯한, 천지를 진동하는
An ear-splitting noise is very loud.

bang [bæŋ] n. 쾅하는 소리; v. 탕 치다, 부딪치다; 쾅 닫(히)다
A bang is a sudden loud noise such as the noise of an explosion.

murder [mə́ːrdər] v. 죽이다, 살해하다; n. 살인
To murder someone means to commit the crime of killing them deliberately.

Build Your Vocabulary

rattle [rætl] v. 왈각달각 소리 내(게 하)다, 덜걱덜걱 움직이다; n. 덜거덕거리는 소리
When something rattles or when you rattle it, it makes short sharp knocking sounds because it is being shaken or it keeps hitting against something hard.

blur [blə:r] n. 흐림, 침침함; 더러움, 얼룩; v. (광경·의식·눈 등을) 흐리게 하다
A blur is a shape or area which you cannot see clearly because it has no distinct outline or because it is moving very fast.

chest [tʃest] ① n. 가슴; 흉곽 ② n. 상자, 궤
Your chest is the top part of the front of your body where your ribs, lungs, and heart are.

flame [fleim] v. 불꽃같이 빛나다; 타오르다; n. 불꽃, 불길
If something flames, it looks red, like it is on fire.

tiara [tiɛ́ərə] n. (여성의) 보석 달린 머리 장식[관]
A tiara is a metal band shaped like half a circle and decorated with jewels which a woman of very high social rank wears on her head at formal social occasions.

necklace [néklis] n. 목걸이
A necklace is a piece of jewelry such as a chain or a string of beads which someone, usually a woman, wears round their neck.

bracelet [bréislit] n. 팔찌
A bracelet is a chain or band, usually made of metal, which you wear around your wrist as jewelry.

ransack [rǽnsæk] vt. 빼앗다; 샅샅이 뒤지다, 들추다; 기억을 더듬다
If people ransack a building, they damage things in it or make it very untidy, often because they are looking for something in a quick and careless way.

burst [bə:rst] v. 갑자기 …하다; 파열하다, 터지다; n. 파열, 돌발
If you burst into tears, laughter, or song, you suddenly begin to cry, laugh, or sing.

pinch [pintʃ] v. (물건·돈을) 훔치다, 슬쩍하다; 꼬집다; n. 꼬집기
To pinch something, especially something of little value, means to steal it.

The Giraffe and the Pelly and Me

bowl over phrasal v. …을 몹시 놀라게 하다, 당황하게 하다; …을 때려눕히다
If you are bowled over by something, you are very impressed or surprised by it.

lung [lʌŋ] n. 폐, 허파
Your lungs are the two organs inside your chest which fill with air when you breathe in.

chorus [kɔ́ːrəs] n. 후렴; 합창, 코러스; v. 합창하다; 이구동성으로 말하다
A chorus is a part of a song which is repeated after each verse.

brilliant [bríljənt] a. 훌륭한, 멋진; 빛나는, 찬란한
A brilliant person, idea, or performance is extremely clever or skilful.

squad car [skwɑ́dkàːr] n. 경찰 순찰차
A squad car is a car used by the police.

villain [vílən] n. 악한, 악인
A villain is someone who deliberately harms other people or breaks the law in order to get what he or she wants.

collar [kɑ́lər] vt. …의 목덜미를 잡다, 체포하다; 깃을[목걸이를] 달다; n. 칼라, 깃
If you collar someone who has done something wrong or who is running away, you catch them and hold them so that they cannot escape.

steady [stédi] vt. 침착하게 하다, 견고하게 하다; a. 고정된, 한결같은, 안정된
If you steady something or if it steadies, it stops shaking or moving about.

pounce [pauns] vi. …에 갑자기 달려들다, 와락 덤벼들다; 비난하다
If someone pounces on you, they come up towards you suddenly and take hold of you.

crouch [krautʃ] v. 몸을 쭈그리다, 쭈그리고 앉다; 웅크리다; n. 웅크림
If you are crouching, your legs are bent under you so that you are close to the ground and leaning forward slightly.

snatch [snætʃ] v. 와락 붙잡다, 잡아채다; n. 잡아 뺏음, 강탈
If you snatch something or snatch at something, you take it or pull it away quickly.

Build Your Vocabulary

drag [dræg] v. 끌(리)다; 느릿느릿 걷다; n. 견인, 끌기
If you drag something, you pull it along the ground.

handcuff [hǽndkʌ̀f] n. (pl.) 수갑, 쇠고랑
Handcuffs are two metal rings which are joined together and can be locked round someone's wrists, usually by the police during an arrest.

wrist [rist] n. 손목
Your wrist is the part of your body between your hand and your arm which bends when you move your hand.

chief [tʃi:f] n. 장(長), 우두머리; a. 최고의, 제1위의
The chief of an organization is the person who is in charge of it.

cat-burglar [kǽtbə́:rglər] n. (2층의 창문으로 침입하는) 밤도둑; 도둑고양이
A cat burglar is a thief who steals from houses or other buildings by climbing up walls and entering through windows or through the roof.

drainpipe [dréinpàip] n. 배수관, 하수관
A drainpipe is a pipe attached to the side of a building, through which rainwater flows from the roof into a drain.

fish [fiʃ] v. 끌어올리다, 꺼내다; 낚시질하다; n. 물고기, 어류
If you fish something out from somewhere, you take or pull it out, often after searching for it for some time.

overcome [òuvərkʌ́m] v. …의 맥을 못 추게 하다; 이기다, 압도하다
If you are overcome by a feeling or event, it is so strong or has such a strong effect that you cannot think clearly.

faint [feint] n. 기절, 졸도; a. 희미한, 어렴풋한; vi. 기절하다
A faint is a spontaneous loss of consciousness.

fearsome [fíərsəm] a. (얼굴 등이) 무시무시한; 무서워하는, 오싹한
Fearsome is used to describe things that are frightening.

servant [sə́:rvənt] n. 하인, 종; 부하
A servant is someone who is employed to work at another person's home.

The Giraffe and the Pelly and Me

patch [pætʃ] n. 헝겊 조각; 반창고; v. 헝겊을 대고 깁다
A patch is a piece of material which you use to cover a hole in something.

mend [mend] v. 고치다, 개선하다; n. 수선, 개량
If you mend something that is broken or not working, you repair it, so that it works properly or can be used.

tyre [taiər] n. (= tire) 타이어
A tyre is a thick piece of rubber which is fitted onto the wheels of vehicles such as cars, buses, and bicycles.

blush [blʌʃ] v. 얼굴을 붉히다, (얼굴이) 빨개지다; n. 얼굴을 붉힘, 홍조
When you blush, your face becomes redder than usual because you are ashamed or embarrassed.

reward [riwɔ́:rd] n. 보상, 보답; v. 보답하다, 보상하다
A reward is something that you are given because you have behaved well.

estate [istéit] n. 소유지, 사유지; 재산
An estate is a large area of land which is owned by a person, family, or organization.

hay [hei] n. 건초, 마초, 건초용 풀
Hay is grass which has been cut and dried so that it can be used to feed animals.

barn [bɑ:rn] n. (농가의) 헛간, 광
A barn is a building on a farm in which crops or animal food can be kept.

desire [dizáiər] n. 욕구, 욕망; v. 몹시 바라다, 요구하다
A desire is a strong wish to do or have something.

install [instɔ́:l] vt. (기기 등을) 장치[설치]하다; 취임시키다
If you install a piece of equipment, you fit it or put it somewhere so that it is ready to be used.

cough [kɔ(:)f] n. 기침; v. 기침하다
A cough is a sudden noisy expulsion of air from the lungs that clears your throat.

Build Your Vocabulary

* **ungrateful** [ʌ̀ŋgréitfəl] a. 은혜를 모르는; 일한 보람 없는, 헛수고의
  If you describe someone as ungrateful, you are criticizing them for not showing thanks or for being unkind to someone who has helped them or done them a favor.

  pushy [púʃi] a. 뻔뻔한, 나서기 잘하는; 진취적인
  If you describe someone as pushy, you mean that they try in a forceful way to get things done as they would like or to increase their status or influence.

* **murmur** [mə́:rmər] v. 중얼거리다; 투덜거리다; n. 중얼거림; 사각사각하는 소리
  If you murmur something, you say it very quietly, so that not many people can hear what you are saying.

* **press** [pres] v. 누르다, 밀어 누르다; 강요하다; n. 누름, 압박; 출판물; 언론
  (pressing a. 긴급한, 절박한)
  If you press something somewhere, you push it firmly against something else.

* **expert** [ékspə:rt] n. 전문가, 숙련가; a. 숙련된, 노련한
  A person who is very skilled at doing something or who knows a lot about a particular subject.

  Geraneous 저자가 만든 기린의 종류
  번역서에는 '사근이 총총' 종이라고 번역되어 있음.

* **variety** [vəráiəti] n. 종류; 변화, 다양(성)
  A variety of something is a type of it.

* **sigh** [sai] v. 한숨 쉬다; n. 한숨, 탄식
  When you sigh, you let out a deep breath, as a way of expressing feelings such as disappointment, tiredness, or pleasure.

* **plantation** [plæntéiʃən] n. 대규모 농원, 대농장, 플랜테이션
  A plantation is a large piece of land, especially in a tropical country, where crops such as rubber, coffee, tea, or sugar are grown.

* **gasp** [gæsp] n. 헐떡거림, 숨 막힘; v. 헐떡거리다, 숨이 막히다
  A gasp is a short quick breath of air that you take in through your mouth, especially when you are surprised, shocked, or in pain.

The Giraffe and the Pelly and Me

* **astonishment** [əstániʃmənt] n. 놀람, 경악
Astonishment is a feeling of great surprise.

* **overwhelm** [òuvərhwélm] vt. 압도하다; 제압하다; 질리게 하다
If you are overwhelmed by a feeling or event, it affects you very strongly, and you do not know how to deal with it.

help yourself idiom (음식 등을) 마음대로 드시오
If you say 'help yourself' to someone, you ask them to take something freely, especially food.

* **saint** [seint] vt. 성인으로 숭배하다; n. 성인, 성자 (sainted a. 성인군자 같은)
Someone who is sainted is considered or officially stated to be a saint.

* **gallop** [gǽləp] v. 전속력으로 달리다, 질주하다; 전속력으로 몰다;
n. 갤럽 (말 등이 전속력으로 달리기)
When a horse gallops, it runs very fast so that all four legs are off the ground at the same time.

whinny [hwíni] v. (말이) 나지막이[기분 좋은 듯이] 울다; n. 말의 울음소리
When a horse whinnies, it makes a series of high-pitched sounds, usually not very loudly.

* **bury** [béri] vt. 묻다; 파묻다, 매장하다
If you bury your head or face in something, you press your head or face into it.

* **blossom** [blásəm] vi. 꽃 피다, 개화하다; n. 꽃
When a tree blossoms, it produces flowers.

pull someone's leg idiom …을 놀리다, 속이다
If you pull someone's leg, you tease them, but not maliciously.

* **arrow** [ǽrou] n. 화살; 화살표
An arrow is a long thin weapon which is sharp and pointed at one end and which often has feathers at the other end.

* **crack** [kræk] v. 깨다, 부수다; 찰칵 소리 내다; 금이 가다;
n. 갈라진 금; 갑작스런 날카로운 소리
When you crack something that has a shell, such as an egg or a nut, you break the shell in order to reach the inside part.

Build Your Vocabulary

guzzle [gʌ́zəl] v. 게걸스럽게 먹다; 폭음하다, 꿀꺽꿀꺽 마시다
If you guzzle something, you drink it or eat it quickly and greedily.

reasonable [ríːzənəbəl] a. 사리를 아는, 분별 있는, 합당한 (reasonably ad. 합당하게)
If you think that someone is fair and sensible you can say that they are reasonable.

haddock [hǽdək] n. [어류] 해덕 (대구의 일종)
Haddock are a type of edible sea fish that are found in the North Atlantic.

cast [kæst] v. (눈·시선을) 던지다; 배정하다; n. 던지기; 깁스
If you cast your eyes or cast a look in a particular direction, you look quickly in that direction.

screech [skriːtʃ] v. 새된 소리를[비명을] 지르다; (자동차 등을) 끽끽 소리 나게 하다; n. 날카로운 외침
When you screech something, you shout it in a loud, unpleasant, high-pitched voice.

tingle [tíŋgəl] v. 따끔따끔 아프다; 설레다; n. 설렘, 흥분; 따끔거림
If you tingle with a feeling such as excitement, you feel it very strongly.

squirrel [skwə́ːrəl] n. 다람쥐
A squirrel is a small animal with a long furry tail.

carpenter [káːrpəntər] n. 목수, 목공
A carpenter is a person whose job is making and repairing wooden things.

choc [tʃɑk] n. (구어) 초콜릿
Choc means chocolate.

nougat [núːgət] n. 누가 (설탕·아몬드 등으로 만든 부드러운 캔디)
Nougat is a kind of firm sweet, containing nuts and sometimes fruit.

aeroplane [ɛ́ərəplèin] n. (= airplane) (영) 비행기
An aeroplane is a vehicle with wings and one or more engines that enable it to fly through the air.

The Giraffe and the Pelly and Me

* **wondrous** [wʌ́ndrəs] a. (시·문어) 놀랄 만한, 불가사의한
If you describe something as wondrous, you mean it is strange and beautiful or impressive.

Gumtwizzler 저자가 만든 과자의 종류

Fizzwinkle 저자가 만든 과자의 종류

Frothblower 저자가 만든 과자의 종류

Spitsizzler 저자가 만든 과자의 종류

Tummytickler 저자가 만든 과자의 종류

Gobwangle 저자가 만든 과자의 종류

Liplicker 저자가 만든 과자의 종류

Plushnugget 저자가 만든 과자의 종류

‡ **sack** [sæk] n. 부대, 자루; vt. 자루에 넣다
Sacks are used to carry or store things such as vegetables or coal.

keep track of idiom …을 놓치지 않고 따라가다
If you keep track of a situation or a person, you make sure that you have the newest and most accurate information about them all the time.

batch [bætʃ] n. 한 솥, 한 차례 굽는 양; vt. 1회분으로 정리[처리]하다
A batch of things is a group of things of the same kind, dealt with at the same time.

Wangdoodle 저자가 만든 과자의 종류

‡ **ripe** [raip] a. 익은, 여문
Ripe fruit or grain is fully grown and ready to eat.

crispy [kríspi] a. 파삭파삭한, 아삭아삭한; 산뜻한
Food that is crispy is pleasantly hard, or has a pleasantly hard surface.

Build Your Vocabulary

* **crust** [krʌst] n. 딱딱한 표면, 겉껍질
  A crust is a hard layer of something.

  Fizzcockler 저자가 만든 과자의 종류

  Nishnobbler 저자가 만든 과자의 종류

  Gumglotter 저자가 만든 과자의 종류

  Bluebubbler 저자가 만든 과자의 종류

  Sherbet Slurper 저자가 만든 과자의 종류

  Tongue Raker 저자가 만든 과자의 종류

* **splendid** [spléndid] a. 멋진, 화려한
  If you say that something is splendid, you mean that it is very good.

  drops [draps] n. 설탕에 향료를 섞어 굳혀 만든 알사탕

* **suck** [sʌk] v. 빨다, 흡수하다; n. 빨아들임
  If you suck something, you hold it in your mouth and pull at it with the muscles in your cheeks and tongue, for example in order to get liquid out of it.

  stickjaw [stíkdʒɔ̀ː] n. (구어) 입안에 붙어 씹기 거북한 캔디[껌·푸딩 등]
  stick (v. 달라붙다) + jaw (n. 턱)

* **talkative** [tɔ́ːkətiv] a. 말이 많은, 수다스러운
  Someone who is talkative talks a lot.

  jujube [dʒúːdʒuːb] n. 대추 젤리; 대추나무, 대추
  Jujube is the name of several types of candy.

* **chilly** [tʃíli] a. 차가운, 쌀쌀한; (태도 등이) 냉담한
  If you feel chilly, you feel rather cold.

* **scarlet** [skáːrlit] a. 주홍[진홍]색의; n. 주홍색, 진홍색
  Something that is scarlet is bright red.

The Giraffe and the Pelly and Me

Scorchdropper 저자가 만든 과자의 종류

label [léibəl] n. 라벨; 브랜드, 상표
A label is a piece of paper or plastic that is attached to an object in order to give information about it.

guarantee [gæ̀rəntí:] vt. 보증하다, 다짐하다; n. 보증, 개런티
If you guarantee something, you promise that it will definitely happen, or that you will do or provide it for someone.

as warm as toast idiom (불을 쬐어) 기분 좋게 따뜻한
Something as warm as toast is very warm and comfortable.

stark [stɑ:rk] ad. 아주, 완전히; a. 황량한; 적나라한
Stark means completely or extremely.

gush [gʌʃ] v. (액체 등이) 분출하다, 내뿜다; 지껄여대다; n. 분출; (감정의) 격발
When liquid gushes out of something, or when something gushes a liquid, the liquid flows out very quickly and in large quantities.

nostril [nástril] n. 콧구멍
Your nostrils are the two openings at the end of your nose.

terrific [tərífik] a. 굉장한, 엄청난; 무서운, 소름이 끼치는
If you describe something or someone as terrific, you are very pleased with them or very impressed by them.

glumptious 사전에 없는 저자가 만든 단어로 '매우 맛있다' 라는 의미

Globgobbler 저자가 만든 과자의 종류

Mecca [mékə] n. 메카 (사우디아라비아 서부의 도시; 마호메트의 탄생지); 성지
Mecca is a city in Saudi Arabia that is the holiest city of Islam, being the place where the Prophet Muhammad was born.

squirt [skwə:rt] v. 분출하다, 뿜어 나오다
If you squirt a liquid somewhere or if it squirts somewhere, the liquid comes out of a narrow opening in a thin fast stream.

Build Your Vocabulary

gullet [gʌ́lit] n. 식도, 목구멍
Your gullet is the tube which goes from your mouth to your stomach.

★ **cascade** [kæskéid] n. (작은) 폭포; v. 폭포가 되어 떨어지다; (폭포처럼) 떨어뜨리다
If you refer to a cascade of something, you mean that there is a large amount of it.

Pishlet 저자가 만든 과자의 종류

nightingale [náitəŋgèil] n. [조류] 나이팅게일
A nightingale is a small brown bird.

drencher [drentʃər] n. 호우, 폭우
drench (vt. 흠뻑 적시다) + ···er (···하는 것)

★ **fiery** [fáiəri] a. 불같은; 불의, 화염의
You can use fiery for emphasis when you are referring to bright colors such as red or orange.

★ **column** [kάləm] n. (연기 등의) 기둥; (신문의) 기고란
A column is something that has a tall narrow shape.

★ **match** [mætʃ] ① n. 성냥 ② vt. 필적하다, 대등하다; 조화하다, 어울리다; n. 상대, 경기
A match is a small wooden stick with a substance on one end that produces a flame when you rub it along the rough side of a matchbox.

★ **roof** [ru:f] n. 지붕; vt. 지붕을 해 덮다
The roof of a building is the covering on top of it that protects the people and things inside from the weather.

look after phrasal v. ···을 보살피다, 돌보다
If you look after someone or something, you do what is necessary to keep them healthy, safe, or in good condition.

★ **melancholy** [mélənkὰli] a. 우울한, 슬픈, 구슬픈; n. 우울(증), 침울
You describe something that you see or hear as melancholy when it gives you an intense feeling of sadness.

★ **farewell** [fὲərwél] n. 작별(인사), 고별; int. 안녕! 잘 가시오!
Farewell means the same as goodbye.

The Giraffe and the Pelly and Me

Comprehension Quiz

Chapters 1 & 2

1. Who was the cleverest farmer?
   A. Farmer Boggis
   B. Farmer Bean
   C. Farmer Bunce

2. Where did Mr. Fox live?
   A. He lived at the top of a tree.
   B. He lived in a hole under Mr. Bean's house.
   C. He lived in a hole under a tree.
   D. He lived in a hole at the bottom of a hill.

3. How did Mr. Fox know where the farmers hid?
   A. He saw the farmers hiding.
   B. He smelled the farmers.
   C. He heard the farmers talking.
   D. He saw the farmer's footprints.

Fantastic Mr. Fox

4. The farmers were angry because _____.

   A. Mr. Fox stole their animals

   B. Mr. Fox dug holes near their farms

   C. they didn't know who stole their animals

   D. they were very poor

5. Mr. Fox went to the farms _____.

   A. in the morning when it was sunny

   B. in the afternoon when it was raining

   C. in the evening when it was dark

   D. at midnight when the farmers were sleeping

Comprehension Quiz

Chapters 3 & 4

1. Mrs. Fox wanted _____ for dinner.
　A. two pigs
　B. three chickens
　C. one turkey
　D. two ducks

2. Put the events in the correct order:
　(　　–　　–　　–　　–　　)
　A. Mr. Fox smelled the air.
　B. Mr. Fox heard a noise.
　C. The farmers shot at Mr. Fox.
　D. Mr. Fox said goodbye to Mrs. Fox.
　E. Mr. Fox saw a gun.

3. Mr. Fox couldn't sleep because _____.
　A. he was hurt
　B. he heard the farmers talking outside
　C. he was very hungry
　D. he wanted to go outside again

Fantastic Mr. Fox

4. What did the farmers do?

   A. They put dogs inside of Mr. Fox's hole.

   B. They dug a hole into Mr. Fox's home.

   C. They shot their guns into Mr. Fox's hole.

   D. They sat outside of Mr. Fox's hole.

5. What did the foxes do when they saw the shovel?

   A. They ran out of the hole.

   B. They hit the shovels with their paws.

   C. They made a new door to get away.

   D. They dug a tunnel.

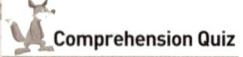
Comprehension Quiz

Chapters 5 & 6

1. Who never washed?
   A. Farmer Bunce
   B. Farmer Bean
   C. Farmer Boggis
   D. Mr. Fox

2. Who drove the tractors?
   A. Farmer Boggis and Farmer Bean
   B. Farmer Bean and Farmer Bunce
   C. Farmer Bunce and Farmer Boggis
   D. Farmer Bean and Mrs. Bean

3. The farmers were so busy, that they _____.
   A. didn't stop to eat lunch
   B. didn't talk to each other
   C. forgot about Mr. Fox
   D. didn't see the people watching

4. Put the events in the correct order: (–   –   –   –)
   A. The farmers got their tractors.
   B. The hill looked like the crater of a volcano.
   C. The people watched the farmers and laughed.

D. Bean had an idea.

E. The farmers started to dig with their mechanical shovels.

5. Match the characters with the quotation:

1. Mr. Fox   A. "You've had your last chicken!"
2. Small Foxes   B. "Tractors! And Mechanical Shovels! Dig for your lives!"
3. Farmer Boggis   C. "I'll pick him up with my bucket. I'll chop him to pieces!"
4. Farmer Bunce   D. "What? I can't hear you. Speak louder."
5. Farmer Bean   E. "What's happening, Dad? What are they doing?"

Comprehension Quiz

Chapters 7 & 8

1. Put the events in the correct order: (– – – –)

A. The farmers took turns sleeping.

B. Farmer Bunce and Farmer Bean turned off their tractors.

C. The farmers ate supper.

D. The farmers sent messages asking for tents, sleeping-bags, and supper.

E. The farmers promised to stay at the hole until they caught the fox.

2. Complete the sentences:

1. The foxes···   A. drank cider.
2. Farmer Boggis···   B. had 6 donuts filled with goose liver paste.
3. Farmer Bunce···   C. ate nothing.
4. Farmer Bean···   D. ate 3 chickens.

3. Mr. Fox knew the farmers were outside of the hole because _____.

A. he smelled Farmer Bean

B. he saw Farmer Boggis

C. he smelled the food and cider

D. he heard the farmers talking

4. What did the farmers do the next day?

   A. They put food inside of the hole.

   B. They dug a bigger hole.

   C. They sat outside of the hole with guns.

   D. They went back to their farms.

5. What problem did the foxes have?

   A. They were cold.

   B. They were hungry.

   C. They couldn't see well in the tunnel.

   D. They were sick.

Comprehension Quiz

Chapters 9 & 10

1. Complete the sentences:

1. Mr. Fox⋯   A. was too weak to dig.
2. The small foxes⋯ B. had an idea.
3. Mrs. Fox⋯   C. waited outside of the hole.
4. The farmers⋯   D. wanted to dig.

2. Why didn't Mr. Fox tell the small foxes where they were going?

A. He wanted to surprise his children.

B. His children would be sad if they didn't get to the place.

C. The place was very scary for small foxes.

D. Mr. Fox wanted the children to stay with Mrs. Fox.

3. Put the events in the correct order:

(–   –   –   –   )

A. Mr. Fox and his children started to dig.

B. Mr. Fox and his children were very excited.

C. The foxes dug downwards and sideways.

D. Mr. Fox pushed up two floor boards.

E. The foxes dug upwards.

Fantastic Mr. Fox

4. What place did Mr. Fox find?

    A. He found a turkey house.

    B. He found a chicken house.

    C. He found Mr. Bean's house.

    D. He found a duck house.

5. What did Mr. Fox take?

    A. He took three hens.

    B. He took two ducks.

    C. He took four turkeys.

    D. He took two hams.

Comprehension Quiz

Chapters 11 & 12

1. **Why did Mrs. Fox close her eye when she saw the small fox?**
   A. She didn't see the hens.
   B. She thought she was dreaming.
   C. She didn't like to eat hens.
   D. She was too weak to keep her eye open.

2. **Why didn't the other animals have food?**
   A. Men with guns would shoot at an animal that tried to leave the hill.
   B. The farmers cut down all of the trees near the hill.
   C. All of the animals were too weak to find food.
   D. The animals could only go outside at night.

3. **Complete the sentence:**

   1. Mrs. Badger··· A. invited Badger, Mole, Rabbit, and Weasel to the feast.
   2. Mrs. Fox··· B. couldn't dig anymore.
   3. Mr. Fox··· C. would help Mr. Fox dig.
   4. Mr. Badger··· D. would tell Mrs. Badger about Fox's Feast.
   5. The Small Badger··· E. was preparing a feast.

Fantastic Mr. Fox

4. Who had six children?

A. Mr. Fox

B. Weasel

C. Rabbit

D. Badger

5. Why did Mr. Fox invite the animals to dinner?

A. He was not very hungry.

B. He teased the other animals.

C. He made the farmers angry.

D. He wanted the animals to dig a new tunnel.

Comprehension Quiz

Chapters 13 & 14

1. What was inside of the storehouse?

   A. Ducks, geese, ham, and bacon

   B. Chickens, ducks, and ham

   C. Cows, chickens, and bread

   D. Ham, cheese, chickens, and geese

2. Who chose the food?

   A. Badger

   B. Mrs. Fox

   C. Mr. Fox

   D. The small foxes

3. Why didn't the animals take all of the food?

   A. The animals were not very hungry.

   B. The animals couldn't carry a lot of food.

   C. The animals didn't want to steal the food.

   D. The animals didn't want the farmers to know that they stole food.

Fantastic Mr. Fox

4. **Put the events in the correct order:**

   (– – – –)

   A. The animals stared at the food.

   B. The two small foxes took the food to Mrs. Fox.

   C. Mr. Fox took four ducks.

   D. The small fox took some carrots.

   E. The animals went into the storehouse.

5. **What did the animals borrow from the farmers?**

   A. They borrowed some hams.

   B. They borrowed a ladder.

   C. They borrowed two push-carts.

   D. They borrowed some cheese.

Comprehension Quiz

Chapters 15 & 16

1. Why was Badger worried?

  A. The animals were stealing.

  B. The animals didn't have much time.

  C. Badger was very hungry.

  D. The animals didn't take enough food.

2. Mr. Fox would _____ if Rat didn't move from the wall.

  A. push Rat

  B. eat Rat

  C. break all of the bricks

  D. yell and make noise

3. Where was the cider cellar?

  A. It was next to Mr. Bunce's house.

  B. It was next to Mr. Bean's house.

  C. It was under Mr. Boggis's house.

  D. It was under Mr. Bean's house.

4. The woman took _____ bottles of cider.

  A. 1   B. 2   C. 3   D. 4

Fantastic Mr. Fox

5. Match the character with the quotation:

1. Rat
2. Badger
3. The smallest fox
4. Mr. Fox

A. "Where are the turkeys? I thought Bean was a turkey man."

B. "Get out and leave me to sip my cider in peace."

C. "We're not after turkeys now. We've got plenty of food."

D. "We take it as medicine—one large glass three times a day and another at bedtime."

Comprehension Quiz

Chapters 17 & 18

1. What did Badger and Mr. Fox sing about?

A. They sang about food.

B. They sang about the farmers.

C. They sang about digging.

D. They sang about their wives.

2. Complete the sentences:

1. There were three···   A. small rabbits.

2. There were four···   B. small badgers.

3. There were five···   C. small weasels.

4. There were six···   D. small moles.

3. Put the events in the correct order: (– – – –)

A. The animals ate the food and didn't talk.

B. Cheering went on for many minutes.

C. Mr. Fox and Badger sang a song.

D. Mr. Fox made a speech.

E. Mr. Fox, Badger, and the smallest fox arrived at the feast.

4. What will the animals do?

A. They will go outside and get more food.

B. They will live inside the farmer's houses.

C. They will live underground and eat the farmer's food.

D. They will show the farmers they are alive.

5. Match the character with the quotation:

1. Badger
2. Farmer Bean
3. Mrs. Fox
4. Farmer Boggis
5. Mr. Fox

A. "And everyday I will go shopping for you all. And everyday we will eat like kings."

B. "He won't stay down there much longer now."

C. "I want you all to stand and drink to our dear friend who saved our lives today...."

D. "He'll be making a dash for it any moment. Keep your guns handy."

E. "My husband is a fantastic fox."

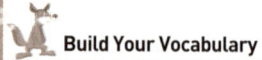
Build Your Vocabulary

1. The Three Farmers

valley [væli] n. 골짜기, 계곡
A valley is a low stretch of land between hills, especially one that has a river flowing through it.

nasty [næsti] a. 더러운, 불쾌한; 심술궂은, 비열한
Something that is nasty is very unpleasant to see, experience, or feel.

mean [mi:n] ① a. 비열한; 성질이 나쁜, 심술궂은 ② vt. 의미하다, 뜻하다
③ a. 평균의, 중간의
If you describe a behavior as mean, you are saying that it is very bad and evil.

enormous [inɔ́:rməs] a. 엄청난, 거대한 (enormously ad. 엄청나게, 거대하게)
You can use enormous to emphasize the great degree or extent of something.

boil [bɔil] ① v. 끓(이)다; 격분하다; n. 끓임, 삶음; ② n. 종기, 부스럼
When a hot liquid boils or when you boil it, bubbles appear in it and it starts to change into steam.

smother [smʌ́ðər] v. 덮어버리다; 숨 막히게 하다, 숨을 막다; n. 연기 나는 것, 혼란
Things that smother something cover it completely.

dumpling [dʌ́mpliŋ] n. 고기만두; 과일 푸딩
Dumplings are small lumps of dough that are cooked and eaten, either with meat and vegetables or as part of a sweet pudding.

goose [gu:s] n. (pl. geese) 거위
A goose is a large bird that has a long neck and webbed feet. Geese are often farmed for their meat.

pot-bellied [pátbèlid] a. 올챙이배의, 배불뚝이의
Someone, usually a man, who is pot-bellied has a round, fat stomach which sticks out.

dwarf [dwɔ:rf] n. 난장이
People who were much smaller than normal were called dwarfs.

Fantastic Mr. Fox

* **chin** [tʃin] n. 아래턱, 턱 끝; v. 턱걸이하다
  Your chin is the part of your face that is below your mouth and above your neck.

* **shallow** [ʃǽlou] n. 물이 얕은 곳, 여울; a. 얕은; 천박한, 얄팍한
  A shallow container, hole, or area of water measures only a short distance from the top to the bottom.

* **liver** [lívər] n. [해부] 간장, 간
  The liver of some animals that is cooked and eaten.

* **mash** [mæʃ] vt. 짓찧다, 짓이기다; n. 짓이긴 것, 갈아서 빻은 것
  If you mash food that is solid but soft, you crush it so that it forms a soft mass.

* **disgusting** [disgʌ́stiŋ] a. 메스꺼운, 역겨운
  If you say that something is disgusting, you are criticizing it because it is extremely unpleasant.

* **paste** [peist] n. 반죽한 것; 풀; v. 풀칠하다, 풀로 붙이다
  Paste is a soft smooth mixture made of crushed meat, fruit, or vegetables.

* **stuff** [stʌf] vt. 채워 넣다, 속을 채우다; n. 물건, 물질
  If you stuff a container or space with something, you fill it with something or with a quantity of things until it is full.

  tummy [tʌ́mi] n. 배
  Your tummy is the part of the front of your body below your waist.

* **ache** [eik] n. 아픔, 쑤심; vi. 아프다, 쑤시다
  An ache is a steady, fairly strong pain in a part of your body.

* **beastly** [bíːstli] a. 짐승 같은; 잔인한; 더러운, 불결한; ad. 몹시, 아주
  If you describe something as beastly, you mean that it is very unpleasant.

* **temper** [témpər] n. 기질, 성질; 화, 노여움
  Your temper is the way you are feeling at a particular time.

* **turkey** [tə́ːrki] n. [조류] 칠면조; 바보, 멍청이
  A turkey is a large bird that is kept on a farm for its meat.

Build Your Vocabulary

* **orchard** [ɔ́ːrtʃərd] n. 과수원
  An orchard is an area of land on which fruit trees are grown.

* **gallon** [gǽlən] n. 갤런 (용량의 단위)
  A gallon is a unit of measurement for liquids that is equal to eight pints.

* **cider** [sáidər] n. (영) 사과술
  Cider is a drink made from apples which in Britain usually contains alcohol.

* **lean** [liːn] ① a. 야윈, 마른 ② v. 상체를 굽히다, 기울(이)다; 기대다, 의지하다
  If you describe someone as lean, you mean that they are thin.

* **crook** [kruk] n. 악한, 사기꾼; 갈고리; v. 구부리다; 굽다
  A crook is a dishonest person or a criminal.

* **nonetheless** [nʌ̀nðəlés] ad. (= nevertheless) 그럼에도 불구하고, 그래도, 역시
  You use nonetheless when saying something that contrasts with what has just been said.

  round about idiom 사방팔방에; 원을 이루어, 둘레에
  Round about means in the area near a place.

2. Mr. Fox

plump [plʌmp] a. 포동포동한, 동그스름한; 속이 가득 찬
You can describe someone or something as plump to indicate that they are rather fat or rounded.

creep [kri:p] vi. 살금살금 걷다, 기다; n. 포복
If something creeps somewhere, it moves very slowly.

rage [reidʒ] n. 격노, 분노; 열광; v. 격노하다; 노하게 하다
Rage is strong anger that is difficult to control.

steal [sti:l] v. (stole-stolen) 훔치다
If you steal something from someone, you take it away from them without their permission and without intending to return it.

shotgun [ʃɑ́tgʌ̀n] n. 새총, 엽총
A shotgun is a gun used for shooting birds and animals which fires a lot of small metal balls at one time.

robber [rɑ́bər] n. 강도, 도둑
A robber is someone who steals money or property from a bank, a shop, or a vehicle, often by using force or threats.

approach [əpróutʃ] v. 접근하다, 다가오다 n. 접근, 가까움
When you approach something, you get closer to it.

lurk [lə:rk] vi. 숨다, 잠복하다; n. 잠복, 밀행
If someone lurks somewhere, they wait there secretly so that they cannot be seen, usually because they intend to do something bad.

dang [dæŋ] n. 'damn(빌어먹을; 젠장)'을 완곡하게 표현한 것
Dang is used by some people to emphasize what they are saying.

blast [blæst] int. 제기랄; n. 센 바람, 돌풍; v. 폭파[발파]하다
Some people say 'blast' to show that they are annoyed at something or someone.

Build Your Vocabulary

lousy [láuzi] a. 형편없는, 저질의; 혐오스러운
If you describe something as lousy, you mean that it is of very bad quality or that you do not like it.

beast [bi:st] n. 야수, 짐승; 짐승 같은 인간
You can refer to an animal as a beast, especially if it is a large, dangerous, or unusual one.

rip [rip] v. 찢다, 벗겨내다; 돌진하다; n. 찢어진 틈, 잡아 찢음
When something rips or when you rip it, you tear it forcefully with your hands or with a tool such as a knife.

gut [gʌt] n. 장, 창자; 용기; 결단력
A person's or animal's guts are all the organs inside them.

blighter [bláitər] n. 녀석; 지독한 놈, 악당
You can call someone who is bad or unpleasant as a blighter.

delicate [délikət] a. 섬세한, 고운; 예민한, 민감한 (delicately ad. 섬세하게)
If something is delicate, it is easy to harm, damage, or break, and needs to be handled or treated carefully.

decent [dí:sənt] a. 적당한; (사회 기준에) 맞는; 점잖은
Decent is used to describe something which is considered to be of an acceptable standard or quality.

bang [bæŋ] n. 쾅하는 소리; v. 탕 치다, 부딪치다; 쾅 닫(히)다
A bang is a sudden loud noise such as the noise of an explosion.

crafty [kræfti] a. 교활한, 간교한
If you describe someone as crafty, you mean that they achieve what they want in a clever way, often by deceiving people.

3. The Shooting

goon [guːn] n. 바보; 불량배
If you call someone a goon, you think they behave in a silly way.

give off phrasal v. (증기·냄새·빛 등을) 발하다, 내다; 방출하다
If something gives off, it produces something else such as heat, light or smoke.

* **filthy** [fílθi] a. 불결한, 더러운
Something that is filthy is very dirty indeed.

* **stink** [stíŋk] n. 악취; v. 악취를 풍기다; 나쁘다
Stink is a strong bad smell.

‡ **rotten** [rátn] a. 썩은; 타락한, 부패한
If food, wood, or another substance is rotten, it has decayed and can no longer be used.

reek [riːk] v. 악취를 풍기다, 냄새가 나다; n. 악취; 연기
To reek of something, usually something unpleasant, means to smell very strongly of it.

‡ **fume** [fjuːm] n. 연기, 김; v. 연기 나다, 그을리다; 노발대발하다
Fumes are the unpleasant and often unhealthy smoke and gases that are produced by fires or by things such as chemicals, fuel, or cooking.

* **poisonous** [pɔ́izənəs] a. 유독[유해]한, 악취를 뿜는
Something that is poisonous will kill you or make you ill if you swallow or absorb it.

cocky [káki] a. 잘난 체하는; 건방진
Someone who is cocky is so confident and sure of their abilities that they annoy other people.

entrance [éntrəns] n. 입구; 입장
The entrance to a place is the way into it, for example a door or gate.

* **crouch** [krautʃ] v. 몸을 쭈그리다, 쪼그리고 앉다; 웅크리다; n. 웅크림
If you are crouching, your legs are bent under you so that you are close to the ground and leaning forward slightly.

Build Your Vocabulary

load [loud] v. …에 장전하다; …에 짐을 싣다; n. 적재 화물; 장전
When someone loads a weapon such as a gun, they put a bullet or missile in it so that it is ready to use.

opposite [ápəzit] a. 반대편의, 맞은편의; 정반대의; n. 정반대의 일; ad. 정반대의 위치에
If one thing is opposite another, it is on the other side of a space from it.

creep [kri:p] vi. (crept-crept) 살금살금 걷다, 기다; n. 포복
If something creeps somewhere, it moves very slowly.

poke [pouk] v. (머리·손가락 등을) 들이대다, 내밀다; 찌르다, 쑤시다
If something pokes out of or through another thing, you can see part of it appearing from behind or underneath the other thing.

sniff [snif] v. 코를 킁킁거리다, 냄새를 맡다; 콧방귀를 뀌다;
n. 킁킁거리며 냄새 맡음; 콧방귀 뀜
When you sniff, you breathe in air through your nose to smell something.

inch [intʃ] v. 조금씩 움직이다; n. 인치 (= 2.54cm); 근소한 거리
To inch somewhere or to inch something somewhere means to move there very slowly and carefully, or to make something do this.

twitch [twitʃ] vi. (손가락·근육 따위가) 씰룩거리다; 홱 잡아당기다, 잡아채다
If a part of your body twitches, or if you twitch it, it makes a sudden quick movement, sometimes one that you cannot control.

scent [sent] n. 냄새, 향기; v. 냄새 맡다; 냄새를 풍기다
The scent of a person or animal is the smell that they leave and that other people sometimes follow when looking for them.

trot [trɑt] v. 빠른 걸음으로 가다; 총총걸음 치다; n. 빠른 걸음
If you trot somewhere, you move fairly fast at a speed between walking and running, taking small quick step.

rustle [rʌ́səl] vi. 바스락거리다, 사랑사랑 소리 내다; n. 바스락거리는 소리
If things such as paper or leaves rustle, or if you rustle them, they move about and make a soft, dry sound.

flatten [flǽtn] vt. 평평하게 하다, 납작하게 하다
If you flatten something or if it flattens, it becomes flat or flatter.

Fantastic Mr. Fox

prick (up) one's ears idiom 귀를 쫑긋 세우다; 열심히 듣다
If an animal pricks its ears, it raises them to listen to a sound.

murky [mə́:rki] a. 어두운, 어두침침한; (어둠·안개가) 짙은
A murky place or time of day is dark and rather unpleasant because there is not enough light.

glint [glint] n. 반짝임, 섬광; v. 반짝이다, 빛나다
A glint is a sudden flash of light or color shining from a bright surface.

speck [spek] n. 작은 반점, 얼룩
A speck is a very small stain, mark, or shape.

polish [páliʃ] v. 닦다, 윤내다; n. 광택; 세련
If you polish something, you rub it with a cloth to make it shine.

Great heavens! idiom 어머나, 야단났네, 저런! (놀람·연민을 나타내는 소리)
People sometimes say 'Great heavens' to express surprise, especially when they are annoyed.

barrel [bǽrəl] n. (총의) 총열; (목재나 금속으로 된 대형) 통, 1 배럴; v. 질주하다
Barrel is the part of a gun that the bullets are fired through.

whip [hwip] n. 채찍(질), 마부; v. 채찍질하다; 급히 움직이다; 휙 잡아채다
A whip is a long thin piece of material such as leather or rope, fastened to a stiff handle.

instant [ínstənt] n. 즉시, 순간; a. 즉각[즉시]의
An instant is an extremely short period of time.

explode [iksplóud] v. 폭발하다, 격발하다; 폭발시키다
If an object such as a bomb explodes or if someone or something explodes it, it bursts loudly and with great force, often causing damage or injury.

float [flout] v. 뜨다; 띄우다; n. 뜨는 물건, 부유물
Something that floats in or through the air hangs in it or moves slowly and gently through it.

Build Your Vocabulary

* **tatter** [tǽtər] v. 해지다; 갈가리 찢다; n. 넝마, 누더기 옷 (tattered a. 해진; 누더기를 두른)
  If something such as clothing or a book is tattered, it is damaged or torn, especially because it has been used a lot over a long period of time.

  blood-stained [blʌ́dstéind] a. 핏자국이 있는; 피투성이의
  blood (n. 피) + stained (a. 얼룩진)

* **toss** [tɔːs] v. 던지다; 흔들리다; n. 던져 올림; 위로 던짐
  If you toss something somewhere, you throw it there lightly, often in a rather careless way.

* **flask** [flæsk] n. 휴대용 병, 플라스크; 보온병
  A flask is a bottle which you use for carrying drinks around with you.

  swig [swig] n. 쭉쭉 들이킴; v. 마구 들이켜다
  A swig is a large and hurried swallow.

* **cider** [sáidər] n. (영) 사과술
  Cider is a drink made from apples which in Britain usually contains alcohol.

* **dig** [dig] v. (dug-dug) 파다, 파헤치다; 찌르다; 탐구하다; n. 파기
  If you dig someone or something out, you get them out of earth or snow, using a shovel or hands.

* **reckon** [rékən] vt. …라고 생각하다; 세다, 계산하다
  If you reckon that something is true, you think that it is true.

* **shovel** [ʃʌ́vəl] n. 삽; v. …을 삽으로 뜨다[파다], 삽으로 일하다
  A shovel is a tool with a long handle that is used for lifting and moving earth, coal, or snow.

Fantastic Mr. Fox

4. The Terrible Shovels

* **tender** [téndər] a. 부드러운; 상냥한, 다정한 (tenderly ad. 부드럽게)
  Someone or something that is tender expresses gentle and caring feelings.

* **lick** [lik] vt. 핥다; n. 전혀 (…이) 없음; 소량; 핥기
  When people or animals lick something, they move their tongue across its surface.

* **stump** [stʌmp] n. 잘리고 남은 부분; (나무의) 그루터기; vt. (발부리를) 차이다
  A stump is a small part of something that remains when the rest of it has been removed or broken off.

* **bleed** [bli:d] v. 피가 나다, 출혈하다
  When you bleed, you lose blood from your body as a result of injury or illness.

* **sweetheart** [swí:thɑ̀:rt] n. (호칭) 여보, 당신; 애인
  You call someone sweetheart if you are very fond of them.

  glum [glʌm] a. 시무룩한, 풀죽은, 침울한
  Someone who is glum is sad and quiet because they are disappointed or unhappy about something.

* **doze** [douz] v. 꾸벅꾸벅 졸다, 선잠을 자다; n. 졸기
  When you doze, you sleep lightly or for a short period, especially during the daytime.

* **frighten** [fráitn] v. 놀라게 하다, 섬뜩하게 하다; 기겁하다 (frightening a. 무서운, 놀라운)
  If something or someone frightens you, they cause you to suddenly feel afraid, anxious, or nervous.

* **scrape** [skreip] v. 긁어내다, 떼다; 문지르다; 스쳐 …에 상처를 내다; n. 긁음; 문지르는 소리
  If you scrape something from a surface, you remove it, especially by pulling a sharp object over the surface.

* **soil** [sɔil] n. 흙, 땅
  Soil is the substance on the surface of the earth in which plants grow.

Build Your Vocabulary

- **quiver** [kwívər] v. (떨리듯) 흔들리다, 떨(리)다; n. 떨기
  If something quivers, it shakes with very small movements.

- **positive** [pázətiv] a. 확신하고 있는; 명확한, 완전한; 긍정적인
  If you are positive about something, you are completely sure about it.

- **sob** [sɑb] v. 흐느껴 울다; n. 흐느낌, 오열
  When someone sobs, they cry in a noisy way, breathing in short breaths.

  scrunch [skrʌntʃ] n. 우두둑 부서지는 소리; vt. (머리를) 헝클어뜨리다
  A scrunch is a loud sound as something is pressed or crushed or as it presses or crushes something else.

- **roof** [ru:f] n. 지붕; vt. 지붕을 해 덮다
  The roof of a building is the covering on top of it that protects the people and things inside from the weather.

- **gather** [gǽðər] v. 모이다, 집결하다; 모으다, 끌다
  If people gather somewhere or if someone gathers people somewhere, they come together in a group.

  crunch [krʌntʃ] n. 우두둑 부서지는 소리; v. 우두둑 깨물다[부수다]
  A crunch is a noisy crackling sound.

- **ceiling** [sí:liŋ] n. 천장; 최고 한도
  A ceiling is the horizontal surface that forms the top part or roof inside a room.

- **awful** [ɔ́:fəl] a. 지독한, 대단한; 무서운; ad. 몹시
  If you look or feel awful, you look or feel ill.

- **electric** [iléktrik] a. 전기(성)의; 전기를 띤
  An electric current, voltage, or charge is one that is produced by electricity.

- **furious** [fjúəriəs] a. 맹렬한, 왕성한; 격노한 (furiously ad. 맹렬히)
  Furious is used to describe something that is done with great energy and effort.

- **slope** [sloup] v. 경사지다, 비탈지다; n. 비탈, 경사
  If a surface slopes, it is at an angle, so that one end is higher than the other.

* **steep** [sti:p] a. 가파른, 험한 (steeply ad. 가파르게)

    A steep slope rises at a very sharp angle and is difficult to go up.

* **gradual** [grǽdʒuəl] a. 점진적인, 단계적인 (gradually ad. 점진적으로)

    A gradual change or process occurs in small stages over a long period of time, rather than suddenly.

* **faint** [feint] a. 희미한, 어렴풋한; vi. 기절하다

    A faint sound, color, mark, feeling, or quality has very little strength or intensity.

* **pant** [pænt] vi. 헐떡거리다, 숨차다; n. 헐떡거림, 숨 가쁨

    If you pant, you breathe quickly and loudly with your mouth open, because you have been doing something energetic.

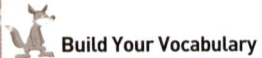
Build Your Vocabulary

5. The Terrible Tractors

- **cross** [krɔːs] a. 기분이 언짢은, 화가 난; 교차한; n. 십자가; v. 교차하다
  Someone who is cross is rather angry or irritated.

- **rotten** [rátn] a. 타락한, 부패한; 썩은
  If you describe something as rotten, you think it is very unpleasant or of very poor quality.

- **give in** phrasal v. 굴복하다, 따르다, 항복하다
  If you give in, you admit that you are defeated or that you cannot do something.

- **string up** phrasal v. 목매달아 죽이다, 교수형에 처하다
  To string someone up means to kill them by hanging them.

- **porch** [pɔːrtʃ] n. (건물 입구에 지붕이 얹혀 있고 흔히 벽이 둘러진) 현관
  A porch is a sheltered area at the entrance to a building. It has a roof and sometimes has walls.

- **pot-bellied** [pátbèlid] a. 올챙이배의, 배불뚝이의
  Someone, usually a man, who is pot-bellied has a round, fat stomach which sticks out.

- **dwarf** [dwɔːrf] n. 난장이
  People who were much smaller than normal were called dwarfs.

- **clog** [klɑg] v. 막히다; 움직임을 방해하다
  When something clogs a hole or place, it blocks it so that nothing can pass through.

- **muck** [mʌk] n. 쓰레기, 오물; 거름, 퇴비; vt. 실패하다, 망쳐놓다
  Muck is dirt or some other unpleasant substance.

- **wax** [wæks] n. 귀지; 밀랍
  Wax is the sticky yellow substance found in your ears.

Fantastic Mr. Fox

stuff [stʌf] n. 물건, 물질; vt. 채워 넣다, 속을 채우다
You can use stuff to refer to things such as a substance, a collection of things, events, or ideas, or the contents of something in a general way without mentioning the thing itself by name.

boil [bɔil] ① n. 종기, 부스럼 ② v. 끓(이)다; 격분하다; n. 끓임, 삶음
A boil is a red, painful swelling on your skin.

itch [itʃ] vi. 가렵다, 근질근질하다; n. 가려움
When a part of your body itches, you have an unpleasant feeling on your skin that makes you want to scratch.

mechanical [məkǽnikəl] a. 기계의, 기계적인
A mechanical device has parts that move when it is working, often using power from an engine or from electricity.

fetch [fetʃ] vt. (가서) 가져오다, 데려오다, 불러오다
If you fetch something or someone, you go and get them from the place where they are.

machinery [məʃíːnəri] n. 기계류; 장치
You can use machinery to refer to machines in general, or machines that are used in a factory or on a farm.

enormous [inɔ́ːrməs] a. 엄청난, 거대한
You can use enormous to emphasize the great degree or extent of something.

caterpillar tractor n. 무한궤도식 트랙터 (상표명)

clank [klæŋk] v. (무거운 쇠붙이 따위가) 절거덕 하고 소리 나다
When large metal objects clank, they make a noise because they are hitting together or hitting against something hard.

murderous [mɔ́ːrdərəs] a. 흉악한; 살인의; 살인적인
Someone who is murderous is likely to murder someone and may already have murdered someone.

brutal [brúːtl] a. 잔인한, 야만적인; 모진, 혹독한
A brutal act or person is cruel and violent.

Build Your Vocabulary

topple [tápəl] vi. 넘어지다, 넘어질 듯 비틀대다
If someone or something topples somewhere or if you topple them, they become unsteady or unstable and fall over.

matchstick [mǽtʃstìk] n. 성냥개비
A matchstick is the wooden part of a match.

★ **deafen** [défən] vt. 귀머거리를 만들다, 귀를 먹먹하게 하다
(deafening a. 귀청이 터질 것 같은)
If a noise deafens you, it is so loud that you cannot hear anything else at the same time.

★ **clang** [klæŋ] v. (무기·종 등이) 쨍그랑 하고 울리다; n. 쨍그랑 하는 소리
When a large metal object clangs, it makes a loud noise.

복습 **bang** [bæŋ] v. 탕 치다, 부딪치다; 쾅 닫(히)다; n. 쾅하는 소리
If something bangs, it makes a sudden loud noise, once or several times.

6. The Race

desperate [déspərit] a. 필사적인; 절망적인, 자포자기의
If you are desperate, you are in such a bad situation that you are willing to try anything to change it.

soil [sɔil] n. 흙, 땅
Soil is the substance on the surface of the earth in which plants grow.

faint [feint] a. 희미한, 어렴풋한; vi. 기절하다
A faint sound, color, mark, feeling, or quality has very little strength or intensity.

crunch [krʌntʃ] n. 우두둑 부서지는 소리; v. 우두둑 깨물다[부수다]
A crunch is a noisy crackling sound.

mighty [máiti] a. 굉장한, 대단한; 강력한, 중대한
Mighty is used to describe something that is very large or powerful.

shovel [ʃʌvəl] n. 삽; v. …을 삽으로 뜨다[파다], 삽으로 일하다
A shovel is a tool with a long handle that is used for lifting and moving earth, coal, or snow.

scrape [skreip] v. 긁어내다, 떼다; 문지르다; 스쳐 …에 상처를 내다; n. 긁음; 문지르는 소리
If you scrape something from a surface, you remove it, especially by pulling a sharp object over the surface.

pant [pænt] vi. 헐떡거리다, 숨차다; n. 헐떡거림, 숨 가쁨
If you pant, you breathe quickly and loudly with your mouth open, because you have been doing something energetic.

catch sight of idiom …을 찾아내다; 언뜻 보다
If you catch sight of someone or something, you suddenly see them.

bucket [bʌkit] n. 양동이, 버킷
A bucket is a round metal or plastic container with a handle attached to its sides.

Build Your Vocabulary

* **chop** [tʃɑp] vt. 자르다, 잘게 썰다
  If you chop something, you cut it into pieces with strong downward movements of a knife or an axe.

* **keen** [kiːn] a. 열심인, 열중하는, 열망하는
  If you are keen on doing something, you very much want to do it.

* **yell** [jel] v. 소리치다, 고함치다; n. 고함소리, 부르짖음
  If you yell, you shout loudly, usually because you are excited, angry, or in pain.

* **lean** [liːn] ① v. 상체를 굽히다, 기울(이)다; 기대다, 의지하다 ② a. 야윈, 마른
  When you lean in a particular direction, you bend your body in that direction.

* **prowl** [praul] vi. 배회하다, (도둑 따위가) 동정을 살피다, 기웃거리다
  If an animal or a person prowls around, they move around quietly, for example when they are hunting.

dwarfish [dwɔ́ːrfiʃ] a. 난쟁이 같은; 유난히 작은
dwarf (n. 난쟁이) + …ish (…의 성질을 가진, …같은)

maniac [méiniæ̀k] n. 미치광이; 열광자; a. 광적인, 광기의
A maniac is a mad person who is violent and dangerous.

* **terrific** [tərífik] a. 굉장한, 엄청난; 무서운, 소름이 끼치는
  If you describe something or someone as terrific, you are very pleased with them or very impressed by them.

* **hop** [hɑp] v. 깡충 뛰다, 뛰어 오르다; n. 깡충깡충 뜀
  If you hop, you move along by jumping.

dervish [dɔ́ːrviʃ] n. 미친 듯이 춤추는 사람; [이슬람교] 수도 탁발승
If you say that someone is like a dervish, you mean that they are turning round and round, waving their arms about, or working very quickly.

* **crater** [kréitər] n. 분화구, (폭발로 생긴) 구멍
  A crater is a very large hole in the ground, which has been caused by something hitting it or by an explosion.

Fantastic Mr. Fox

* **volcano** [vɑlkéinou] n. 화산; 분화구
  A volcano is a mountain from which hot melted rock, gas, steam, and ash from inside the earth sometimes burst.

* **extraordinary** [ikstrɔ́:rdənèri] a. 비상한, 비범한, 예사롭지 않은
  If you describe something as extraordinary, you mean that it is very unusual or surprising.

* **rush** [rʌʃ] v. 서두르다, 돌진하다; 급습[돌격]하다
  If you rush somewhere, you go there quickly.

* **jeer** [dʒiər] vi. 조소하다, 야유하다; n. 조롱, 희롱
  To jeer at someone means to say or shout rude and insulting things to them to show that you do not like or respect them.

* **obstinate** [ábstənit] a. 완고한, 고집 센
  If you describe someone as obstinate, you are being critical of them because they are very determined to do what they want, and refuse to change their mind or be persuaded to do something else.

* **determined** [ditə́:rmind] a. 결연한, 굳게 결심한
  If you are determined to do something, you have made a firm decision to do it and will not let anything stop you.

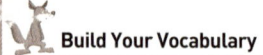

Build Your Vocabulary

7. "We'll Never Let Him Go"

switch [switʃ] v. 스위치를 넣다[돌리다]; n. 스위치
If you switch off a light or other electrical device, you stop it working by operating a switch.

stiff [stif] a. 굳은, 뻣뻣한; 완강한, 완고한
Something that is stiff is firm or does not bend easily.

rage [reidʒ] n. 격노, 분노; 열광; v. 격노하다; 노하게 하다
Rage is strong anger that is difficult to control.

curse [kəːrs] vt. 저주하다, 욕설을 퍼붓다; n. 저주, 악담
If you curse, you use rude or offensive language, usually because you are angry about something.

waddle [wádl] vi. 뒤뚱거리며 걷다, 흔들 흔들거리며 가다; n. 뒤뚱거리는 걸음걸이
To waddle somewhere means to walk there with short, quick steps, swinging slightly from side to side.

filthy [fílθi] a. 불결한, 더러운
Something that is filthy is very dirty indeed.

stink [stíŋk] n. 악취; v. 악취를 풍기다; 나쁘다 (stinking a. 악취가 나는)
Stink is a strong bad smell.

what the heck idiom (= what the hell) 도대체 무엇[왜] (비속어)
You use the heck in expressions such as 'what the heck' in order to emphasize a question, especially when you are puzzled or annoyed.

declare [diklέər] v. 선언하다; 단언하다
If you declare that something is true, you say that it is true in a firm, deliberate way.

dingbat [díŋbæt] n. (속어) 바보, 미치광이
A dingbat is a silly empty-headed person.

swear [swɛ́ər] v. (swore–sworn) 맹세하다, 단언하다; 욕을 하다; n. 맹세, 선서
If you swear to do something, you promise in a serious way that you will do it.

Fantastic Mr. Fox

* **solemn** [sáləm] a. 엄숙한, 근엄한
Someone or something that is solemn is very serious rather than cheerful or humorous.

* **oath** [ouθ] n. 맹세, 서약
An oath is a formal promise, especially a promise to be loyal to a person or country.

복습 **fetch** [fetʃ] vt. (가서) 가져오다, 데려오다, 불러오다
If you fetch something or someone, you go and get them from the place where they are.

* **miserable** [mízərəbəl] a. 비열한, 치사한; 불행한, 비참한; 초라한
If you describe someone as miserable, you mean that you do not like them because they are bad-tempered or unfriendly.

midget [mídʒit] n. 난쟁이, 꼬마; a. 보통보다 작은, 극소형의
People who are very short are sometimes referred to as midgets.

* **sickly** [síkli] a. 혐오스러운, 불쾌한; 병약한, 자주 앓는; ad. 병적으로
A sickly smell or taste is unpleasant and makes you feel slightly sick.

* **scarlet** [skáːrlit] a. 주홍[진홍]색의; n. 주홍색, 진홍색
Something that is scarlet is bright red.

gum [gum] ① n. 잇몸, 치은 ② n. 고무질, 점성 고무
Your gums are the areas of firm, pink flesh inside your mouth, which your teeth grow out of.

* **starve** [staːrv] v. 굶주리다, 굶어죽다; 갈망하다
If people starve, they suffer greatly from lack of food which sometimes leads to their death.

sleeping-bag [slíːpiŋbæg] n. 침낭
A sleeping-bag is a large deep bag with a warm lining, used for sleeping in, especially when you are camping.

Build Your Vocabulary

8. The Foxes Begin to Starve

boil [bɔil] ① v. 끓(이)다; 격분하다; n. 끓임, 삶음 ② n. 종기, 부스럼
When a hot liquid boils or when you boil it, bubbles appear in it and it starts to change into steam.

smother [smʌ́ðər] v. 덮어버리다; 숨 막히게 하다, 숨을 막다; n. 연기 나는 것, 혼란
Things that smother something cover it completely.

dumpling [dʌ́mpliŋ] n. 고기만두; 과일 푸딩
Dumplings are small lumps of dough that are cooked and eaten, either with meat and vegetables or as part of a sweet pudding.

disgusting [disgʌ́stiŋ] a. 메스꺼운, 역겨운
If you say that something is disgusting, you are criticizing it because it is extremely unpleasant.

goose [gu:s] n. (pl. geese) 거위
A goose is a large bird that has a long neck and webbed feet. Geese are often farmed for their meat.

liver [lívər] n. [해부] 간장, 간
The liver of some animals that is cooked and eaten.

paste [peist] n. 반죽한 것; 풀; v. 풀칠하다, 풀로 붙이다
Paste is a soft smooth mixture made of crushed meat, fruit, or vegetables.

gallon [gǽlən] n. 갤런 (용량의 단위)
A gallon is a unit of measurement for liquids that is equal to eight pints.

cider [sáidər] n. (영) 사과술
Cider is a drink made from apples which in Britain usually contains alcohol.

steam [sti:m] v. 증기가 발생하다; (식품 등을) 찌다; n. 증기 (steaming a. 김이 나는)
If something steams, it gives off steam.

tender [téndər] a. 부드러운; 상냥한, 다정한
Meat or other food that is tender is easy to cut or chew.

Fantastic Mr. Fox

- **scent** [sent] n. 냄새, 향기; v. 냄새 맡다; 냄새를 풍기다
  The scent of a person or animal is the smell that they leave and that other people sometimes follow when looking for them.

- **waft** [wɑːft] v. 둥둥 떠돌다, 둥실둥실 실어 나르다
  If sounds or smells waft through the air, or if something such as a light wind wafts them, they move gently through the air.

- **crouch** [krautʃ] v. 몸을 쭈그리다, 쪼그리고 앉다; 웅크리다; n. 웅크림
  If you are crouching, your legs are bent under you so that you are close to the ground and leaning forward slightly.

- **sneak** [sniːk] v. 살금살금 돌아다니다; 슬쩍 넣다[집다]; 고자질하다; n. 밀고자
  If you sneak somewhere, you go there very quietly on foot, trying to avoid being seen or heard.

- **snatch** [snætʃ] v. 와락 붙잡다, 잡아채다; n. 잡아 뺏음, 강탈
  If you snatch something or snatch at something, you take it or pull it away quickly.

- **dare** [dɛər] v. 감히 …하다; 무릅쓰다; 도전하다
  If you say to someone 'don't you dare' do something, you are telling them not to do it and letting them know that you are angry.

- **headlamp** [hédlæ̀mp] n. (= headlight) 헤드라이트, 전조등
  A vehicle's headlamps are the large powerful lights at the front.

- **shone** [ʃoun] v. 'shine(비추다)'의 과거·과거분사
  Shone is the past tense and past participle of shine.

- **dig** [dig] v. 파다, 파헤치다; 찌르다; 탐구하다; n. 파기
  If you dig one thing into another or if one thing digs into another, the first thing is pushed hard into the second, or presses hard into it.

- **flick** [flik] vt. 가볍게 치다, 튀기다; n. 가볍게 치기
  If you flick something away, or off something else, you remove it with a quick movement of your hand or finger.

- **hatchet** [hǽtʃit] n. 손도끼
  A hatchet is a small axe that you can hold in one hand.

Build Your Vocabulary

* **pistol** [pístl] n. 권총, 피스톨
  A pistol is a small gun which is held in and fired from one hand.

* **weapon** [wépən] n. 무기, 흉기
  A weapon is an object such as a gun, a knife, or a missile, which is used to kill or hurt people in a fight or a war.

* **stool** [stu:l] n. (등이 없는) 걸상; 발판
  A stool is a seat with legs but no support for your arms or back.

* **creep** [kri:p] vi. 살금살금 걷다, 기다; n. 포복
  If something creeps somewhere, it moves very slowly.

* **sniff** [snif] n. 킁킁거리며 냄새 맡음; 콧방귀 뀜; v. 코를 킁킁거리다, 냄새를 맡다; 콧방귀를 뀌다
  Sniff is a smelling by taking short breaths through the nose.

9. Mr. Fox Has a Plan

sip [sip] n. 한 모금, 한 번 마심; vt. 찔끔찔끔 마시다
A sip is a small amount of drink that you take into your mouth.

make a dash for idiom …을 향해 돌진하다
If you make a dash for a place, you run there very quickly, for example to escape from someone or something.

snap [snæp] v. 날카롭게[느닷없이] 말하다; 덥석 물다; 홱 잡다; 짤깍 소리 내다; n. 툭 소리 냄
If someone snaps at you, they speak to you in a sharp, unfriendly way.

desperate [déspərit] a. 필사적인; 절망적인, 자포자기의 (desperately a. 필사적으로)
If you are desperate, you are in such a bad situation that you are willing to try anything to change it.

stir [stəːr] v. 휘젓다, 움직이다; n. 움직임; 휘젓기
If you stir, you move slightly, for example because you are uncomfortable or beginning to wake up.

get to one's feet idiom 일어서다
If you get to your feet, you stand up.

undefeated [ʌ̀ndifíːtid] a. 진 적이 없는, 무패의
If a sports player or team is undefeated, nobody has beaten them over a particular period of time.

suffer [sʌ́fər] v. (고통·상해·손해·슬픔 등을) 겪다; 고통을 겪다
If you suffer something bad, you are in a situation in which something painful, harmful, or very unpleasant happens to you.

Build Your Vocabulary

10. Boggis's Chicken House Number One

marvellous [máːrvələs] a. 훌륭한, 우수한; 놀라운, 믿기 어려운
If you describe someone or something as marvellous, you are emphasizing that they are very good.

describe [diskráib] vt. 묘사하다, 기술하다; 평하다
If you describe a person, object, event, or situation, you say what they are like or what happened.

murky [mə́ːrki] a. 어두운, 어두침침한; (어둠·안개가) 짙은
A murky place or time of day is dark and rather unpleasant because there is not enough light.

peep [piːp] n. 엿봄, 훔쳐보기, 슬쩍 봄; vi. 엿보다, 슬쩍 들여다보다
A peep is a quick look at something, often secretly and quietly.

weary [wíəri] a. 피로한, 지친 (wearily ad. 지쳐서, 지친 상태로)
If you are weary, you are very tired.

slope [sloup] v. 경사지다, 비탈지다; n. 비탈, 경사
If a surface slopes, it is at an angle, so that one end is higher than the other.

plank [plæŋk] n. 널, 두꺼운 판자
A plank is a long, flat, rectangular piece of wood.

peek [piːk] n. 엿봄; vi. 살짝 들여다보다, 엿보다
A peek is a quick look at something, often secretly.

creak [kriːk] v. 삐걱삐걱 소리를 내며 움직이(게 하)다; n. 삐걱거리는 소리
If something creaks, it makes a short, high-pitched sound when it moves.

duck [dʌk] ① v. 피하다; 물속으로 들어가다; 머리를 홱 숙이다 ② n. 오리
If you duck, you move your head or the top half of your body quickly downwards to avoid something that might hit you, or to avoid being seen.

awful [ɔ́ːfəl] a. 지독한, 대단한; 무서운; ad. 몹시
If you look or feel awful, you look or feel ill.

Fantastic Mr. Fox

- **cautious** [kɔ́:ʃəs] a. 조심성 있는, 신중한 (cautiously ad. 조심스럽게)
Someone who is cautious acts very carefully in order to avoid possible danger.

- **poke** [pouk] v. (머리·손가락 등을) 들이대다, 내밀다; 찌르다, 쑤시다
If something pokes out of or through another thing, you can see part of it appearing from behind or underneath the other thing.

- **gap** [gæp] n. 갈라진 틈, 구멍; 큰 차이, 격차
A gap is a space between two things or a hole in the middle of something solid.

- **shriek** [ʃri:k] n. 비명; v. 새된 소리를 지르다, 비명을 지르다
A shriek is a short, very loud cry.

- **yell** [jel] v. 소리치다, 고함치다; n. 고함소리, 부르짖음
If you yell, you shout loudly, usually because you are excited, angry, or in pain.

- **prance** [præns] vi. 여기저기 뛰어 다니다, 껑충거리며 나아가다; n. (말의) 날뛰기; 활보
If someone prances around, they walk or move around with exaggerated movements, usually because they want people to look at them and admire them.

- **hallelujah** [hæ̀ləlú:jə] int. 할렐루야 (기쁨의 외침)

- **hooray** [hu(:)réi] int. 만세; vi. 만세를 부르다
People sometimes shout 'Hooray!' when they are very happy and excited about something.

- **scramble** [skrǽmbəl] v. 기어오르다; 서로 (다투어) 빼앗다; 뒤섞다; n. 기어오르기
If you scramble over rocks or up a hill, you move quickly over them or up it using your hands to help you.

- **shed** [ʃed] n. 헛간, 창고
A shed is a small building that is used for storing things such as garden tools.

- **teem** [ti:m] ① vi. 충만하다, 풍부하다, 비옥하다 ② vt. (그릇을) 비우다
If you say that a place is teeming with people or animals, you mean that it is crowded and the people and animals are moving around a lot.

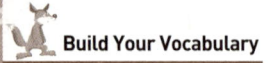
Build Your Vocabulary

aim [eim] v. …을 겨냥하다, 목표삼다; n. 겨냥, 조준; 목적, 뜻
If you aim at something or aim to do something, you plan or hope to achieve it.

trough [trɔ(:)f] n. 구유, 여물통
A trough is a long narrow container from which farm animals drink or eat.

lap up phrasal v. 핥아[마셔]버리다
When an animal laps up a drink, it uses short quick movements of its tongue to take liquid up into its mouth.

plump [plʌmp] a. 포동포동한, 둥그스름한; 속이 가득 찬
You can describe someone or something as plump to indicate that they are rather fat or rounded.

hen [hen] n. 암탉; 암평아리
A hen is a female chicken.

jaw [dʒɔ:] n. 턱, 아래턱
A person's or animal's jaws are the two bones in their head which their teeth are attached to.

instant [ínstənt] a. 즉각[즉시]의; n. 즉시, 순간 (instantly ad. 당장에, 즉각)
You use instant to describe something that happens immediately.

fool around phrasal v. 빈둥거리며 세월을 보내다
If you fool around, you behave in a silly, dangerous, or irresponsible way.

feast [fi:st] n. 축제; 대접; 진수성찬; v. 축연을 베풀다; 진수성찬을 먹다
A feast is a large and special meal.

jiffy [dʒífi] n. 잠시, 순간
If you say that you will do something in a jiffy, you mean that you will do it very quickly or very soon.

arrangement [əréindʒmənt] n. 배열, 조정, 준비; 정돈, 정리
Arrangements are plans and preparations which you make so that something will happen or be possible.

Fantastic Mr. Fox

11. A Surprise for Mrs. Fox

explode [iksplóud] v. 폭발하다, 격발하다; 폭발시키다
If an object such as a bomb explodes or if someone or something explodes it, it bursts loudly and with great force, often causing damage or injury.

burst [bə:rst] v. 갑자기 …하다; 파열하다, 터지다; n. 파열, 돌발
To burst into or out of a place means to enter or leave it suddenly with a lot of energy or force.

murmur [mə́:rmər] v. 중얼거리다; 투덜거리다; n. 중얼거림; 사각사각하는 소리
If you murmur something, you say it very quietly, so that not many people can hear what you are saying.

starve [stɑ:rv] v. 굶주리다, 굶어죽다; 갈망하다
If people starve, they suffer greatly from lack of food which sometimes leads to their death.

splutter [splʌ́tər] v. 흥분하여 말하다; 푸푸 소리를 내다, 푹푹 내뿜다
If someone splutters, they make short sounds and have difficulty speaking clearly, for example because they are embarrassed or angry.

pluck [plʌk] v. 잡아 뜯다, 뽑다; n. 잡아 뜯기; 담력, 용기
If you pluck something from somewhere, you take it between your fingers and pull it sharply from where it is.

as easy as pie idiom 아주 쉬운, 퍽 간단한
Something as easy as pie is very easy to do.

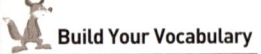

12. Badger

badger [bǽdʒər] n. [동물] 오소리
A badger is a wild animal which has a white head with two wide black stripes on it. Badgers live underground and usually come up to feed at night.

whacking [hwǽkiŋ] a. 큰, 굉장한
You can use whacking to emphasize how big something is.

churgle 사전에 없는 저자가 합성한 단어
chuckle (vi. 킬킬 웃다) + gurgle (v. 목을 꿀꺽거리다)

peek [pi:k] n. 엿봄; vi. 살짝 들여다보다, 엿보다
A peek is a quick look at something, often secretly.

roof [ru:f] n. 지붕; vt. 지붕을 해 덮다
The roof of a building is the covering on top of it that protects the people and things inside from the weather.

furry [fə́:ri] a. 털로 덮인, 부드러운 털의
If you describe something as furry, you mean that it has a soft rough texture like fur.

foggy [fɔ́(:)gi] a. (생각 등이) 몽롱한; 안개가 자욱한; 침침한, 흐린
If you say that you haven't the foggiest or you haven't the foggiest idea, you are emphasizing that you do not know something.

ceiling [sí:liŋ] n. 천장; 최고 한도
A ceiling is the horizontal surface that forms the top part or roof inside a room.

chaos [kéiɑs] n. 혼돈, 대혼란, 무질서
Chaos is a state of complete disorder and confusion.

countryside [kʌ́ntrisàid] n. 한 지방, 시골
The countryside is land which is away from towns and cities.

mole [moul] n. [동물] 두더지
A mole is a small animal with black fur that lives underground.

Fantastic Mr. Fox

weasel [wíːzəl] n. [동물] 족제비; 밀고자
A weasel is a small wild animal with a long thin body, a tail, short legs, and reddish-brown fur.

sneak [sniːk] v. 살금살금 돌아다니다; 슬쩍 넣다[집다]; 고자질하다; n. 밀고자
If you sneak somewhere, you go there very quietly on foot, trying to avoid being seen or heard.

furious [fjúəriəs] a. 맹렬한, 왕성한; 격노한 (furiously ad. 맹렬히)
Furious is used to describe something that is done with great energy and effort.

paw [pɔː] n. (동물·갈고리 발톱이 있는) 발; v. 앞발로 차다
The paws of an animal such as a cat, dog, or bear are its feet, which have claws for gripping things and soft pads for walking on.

tease [tiːz] v. 놀리다, 괴롭히다; 졸라대다; n. 골리기
To tease someone means to laugh at them or make jokes about them in order to embarrass, annoy, or upset them.

galore [gəlɔ́ːr] a. (명사 뒤에 쓰여) 많은, 풍부한
You use galore to emphasize that something you like exists in very large quantities.

spread [spred] v. 퍼뜨리다, 확산시키다; 펴다; n. 퍼짐, 폭, 넓이
If something spreads or is spread by people, it gradually reaches or affects a larger and larger area or more and more people.

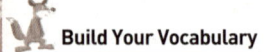

Build Your Vocabulary

13. Bunce's Giant Storehouse

- **painful** [péinfəl] a. 고통스러운, 괴로운; 아픈
  Situations, memories, or experiences that are painful are difficult and unpleasant to deal with, and often make you feel sad and upset.

- **subject** [sʌ́bdʒikt] n. 주제; 학과; 백성, 국민; a. 영향을 받는; vt. 복종[종속]시키다
  The subject of something such as a conversation, letter, or book is the thing that is being discussed or written about.

- **dig** [dig] v. 파다, 파헤치다; 찌르다; 탐구하다; n. 파기
  If you dig one thing into another or if one thing digs into another, the first thing is pushed hard into the second, or presses hard into it.

- **terrific** [tərífik] a. 굉장한, 엄청난; 무서운, 소름이 끼치는
  If you describe something or someone as terrific, you are very pleased with them or very impressed by them.

- **pace** [peis] n. 걸음걸이; 속도; v. 왔다 갔다 하다, 천천히 걷다
  Your pace is the speed at which you walk.

- **crouch** [krautʃ] v. 몸을 쭈그리다, 쪼그리고 앉다; 웅크리다; n. 웅크림
  If you are crouching, your legs are bent under you so that you are close to the ground and leaning forward slightly.

- **grin** [grin] v. 이를 드러내고 싱긋 웃다; n. 싱긋 웃음
  When you grin, you smile broadly.

- **sly** [slai] a. 은밀한, 음흉한; 익살맞은 (slyly ad. 음흉하게)
  A sly look or expression shows that you know something that other people do not know.

- **belong** [bilɔ́(:)ŋ] vi. (…에) 속하다, (…의) 소유물이다; 소속하다
  If something belongs to you, you own it.

- **nasty** [nǽsti] a. 더러운, 불쾌한; 심술궂은, 비열한
  Something that is nasty is very unpleasant to see, experience, or feel.

Fantastic Mr. Fox

pot-bellied [pátbèlid] a. 올챙이배의, 배불뚝이의
Someone, usually a man, who is pot-bellied has a round, fat stomach which sticks out.

dwarf [dwɔːrf] n. 난장이
People who were much smaller than normal were called dwarfs.

goose [guːs] n. (pl. geese) 거위
A goose is a large bird that has a long neck and webbed feet. Geese are often farmed for their meat.

lick [lik] vt. 핥다; (불길이) 넘실거리다; n. 전혀 (…이) 없음; 소량; 핥기
When people or animals lick something, they move their tongue across its surface.

tender [téndər] a. 부드러운; 상냥한, 다정한
Meat or other food that is tender is easy to cut or chew.

blindfold [bláindfòuld] a. 눈을 가리고; v. 눈을 가리다; 속이다; n. 눈가리개; 눈 속임수
If you say that you can do something blindfold, you are emphasizing that you can do it easily.

gap [gæp] n. 갈라진 틈, 구멍; 큰 차이, 격차
A gap is a space between two things or a hole in the middle of something solid.

smack [smæk] ad. 정면으로; v. 입맛을 다시다, 혀를 차다; 찰싹 치다; n. 찰싹 하는 소리; 입맛 다심
Something that is smack in a particular place is exactly in that place.

bull's eye [búlzài] n. 중심, 정곡(正鵠); 적중, 명중
If something that you do or say hits the bull's eye, it has exactly the effect that you intended it to have.

scramble [skræmbəl] v. 기어오르다; 서로 (다투어) 빼앗다; 뒤섞다; n. 기어오르기
If you scramble over rocks or up a hill, you move quickly over them or up it using your hands to help you.

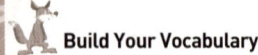

Build Your Vocabulary

- **gape** [geip] vi. (놀람·감탄으로) 입을 딱 벌리다; 크게 갈라지다; n. 갈라진 틈; 입을 딱 벌림
  If you gape, you look at something in surprise, usually with an open mouth.

- **overwhelm** [òuvərhwélm] vt. 압도하다, 제압하다; 질리게 하다
  If you are overwhelmed by a feeling or event, it affects you very strongly, and you do not know how to deal with it.

- **proclaim** [proukléim] vt. 선언하다, 공포하다, 성명하다
  If you proclaim something, you say publicly or officially that something important is true or exist.

- **mighty** [máiti] a. 굉장한, 대단한; 강력한, 중대한
  Mighty is used to describe something that is very large or powerful.

- **stuff** [stʌf] n. 물건, 물질; vt. 채워 넣다, 속을 채우다
  You can use stuff to refer to things such as a substance, a collection of things, events, or ideas, or the contents of something in a general way without mentioning the thing itself by name.

- **stack** [stæk] v. 쌓다, 쌓아올리다; n. 더미; 많음, 다량
  If you stack a number of things, you arrange them in neat piles.

- **cupboard** [kʌ́bərd] n. 식기장, 찬장
  A cupboard is a piece of furniture that has one or two doors, usually contains shelves, and is used to store things.

- **roast** [roust] v. 굽다, 그을리다, 뜨겁게 하다
  When you roast meat or other food, you cook it by dry heat in an oven or over a fire.

- **dangle** [dǽŋgəl] v. (달랑달랑) 매달(리)다; n. 매달린 것
  If something dangles from somewhere or if you dangle it somewhere, it hangs or swings loosely.

- **rafter** [rǽftər] n. [건축] 서까래
  Rafters are the sloping pieces of wood that support a roof.

feast [fiːst] v. 축연을 베풀다; 진수성찬을 먹다; n. 축제; 대접; 진수성찬
If you feast on a particular food, you eat a large amount of it with great enjoyment.

grub [grʌb] n. (구어) 음식; 땅벌레, 굼벵이; v. 개간하다; 땅을 파헤치다
Grub is food.

release [rilíːs] vt. 놓아 주다, 방출하다; 풀어 주다, 석방하다; n. 석방
If you release someone or something, you stop holding them.

ravenous [rǽvənəs] a. 몹시 굶주린; 게걸스럽게 먹는 (ravenously ad. 굶주려서)
If you are ravenous, you are extremely hungry.

luscious [lʌ́ʃəs] a. 감미로운, 달콤한
Luscious food is juicy and very good to eat.

lick one's chops idiom 입맛을 다시다
If you lick your chops, you move your tongue over your lips, especially before eating something good.

prowl [praul] vi. 배회하다, (도둑 따위가) 동정을 살피다, 기웃거리다
If an animal or a person prowls around, they move around quietly, for example when they are hunting.

thread [θred] n. 실처럼 가느다란 것; 바느질 실; vt. 실을 꿰다
A thread of something such as liquid, light, or color is a long thin line or piece of it.

saliva [səláivə] n. 침, 타액
Saliva is the watery liquid that forms in your mouth and helps you to chew and digest food.

jaw [dʒɔː] n. 턱, 아래턱
A person's or animal's jaws are the two bones in their head which their teeth are attached to.

suspend [səspénd] v. 매달다, 걸다; 중지하다
If something is suspended from a high place, it is hanging from that place.

Build Your Vocabulary

mid-air [midέər] n. 공중
If something happens in mid-air, it happens in the air, rather than on the ground.

snap [snæp] v. 덥석 물다; 홱 잡다; 짤깍 소리 내다; 날카롭게[느닷없이] 말하다; n. 툭 소리 냄
If an animal such as a dog snaps at you, it opens and shuts its jaws quickly near you, as if it were going to bite you.

neat [ni:t] a. 산뜻한, 깔끔한
A neat place, thing, or person is tidy and smart, and has everything in the correct place.

tidy [táidi] a. 단정한, 말쑥한, 깔끔한; v. 치우다, 정돈하다
Something that is tidy is neat and is arranged in an organized way.

choice [tʃɔis] a. (choicer–choicest) (음식 따위가) 특상의, 고급의
Choice means of very high quality.

morsel [mɔ́:rsəl] n. 소량, 조금; 한 입, 한 조각; 가벼운 식사
A morsel is a very small amount of something, especially a very small piece of food.

plump [plʌmp] a. 포동포동한, 둥그스름한; 속이 가득 찬
You can describe someone or something as plump to indicate that they are rather fat or rounded.

adore [ədɔ́:r] vt. 숭배하다, 아주 좋아하다
If you adore someone, you feel great love and admiration for them.

fetch [fetʃ] vt. (가서) 가져오다, 데려오다, 불러오다
If you fetch something or someone, you go and get them from the place where they are.

step-ladder [stepl金dər] n. 발판 사다리, 접사다리
A step-ladder is a ladder that is hinged in the middle.

magnificent [mægnífəsənt] a. 웅장한, 장엄한, 훌륭한
If you say that something or someone is magnificent, you mean that you think they are extremely good, beautiful, or impressive.

Fantastic Mr. Fox

twerp [twəːrp] n. (속어) 시시한 놈, 바보 녀석
If you call someone a twerp, you are insulting them and saying that they are silly or stupid.

thoughtful [θɔ́ːtfəl] a. 생각이 깊은, 사려 깊은
If you describe someone as thoughtful, you approve of them because they remember what other people want, need, or feel, and try not to upset them.

fellow [félou] n. 친구, 동료
You use fellow to describe people who are in the same situation as you, or people you feel you have something in common with.

bunch [bʌntʃ] n. 다발, 송이; 다량; 떼, 한패
A bunch of things is a number of things, especially a large number.

heap [hiːp] n. 더미, 쌓아올린 것; 덩어리
A heap of things is a pile of them, especially a pile arranged in a rather untidy way.

twitch [twitʃ] vi. (손가락·근육 따위가) 씰룩거리다; 홱 잡아당기다, 잡아채다
If a part of your body twitches, or if you twitch it, it makes a sudden quick movement, sometimes one that you cannot control.

push-cart [púʃkàːrt] n. 미는 손수레; 유모차
A push-cart is a type of cart that is pushed.

load [loud] v. …에 짐을 싣다; …에 장전하다; n. 적재 화물; 장전
If you load a vehicle or a container, you put a large quantity of things into it.

trolley [tráli] n. (영) 손수레
A trolley is an object with wheels that you use to transport heavy things such as shopping or luggage.

rush [rʌʃ] v. 서두르다, 돌진하다; 급습[돌격]하다
If you rush somewhere, you go there quickly.

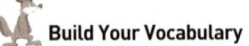

Build Your Vocabulary

14. Badger Has Doubts

steal [stiːl] v. 훔치다
If you steal something from someone, you take it away from them without their permission and without intending to return it.

dotty [dáti] a. 머리가 돈; 점이 있는; 점 같은
If you say that someone is dotty, you mean that they are slightly mad or likely to do strange things.

frump [frʌmp] n. 수수한 사람; 지저분한 여자
Frump is somebody who is unattractive.

swipe [swaip] v. 훔치다; 힘껏 치다; 벌떡벌떡 들이켜다; n. 강타; 맹타; 비난
If you swipe something, you steal it quickly.

starve [stɑːrv] v. 굶주리다, 굶어죽다; 갈망하다
If people starve, they suffer greatly from lack of food which sometimes leads to their death.

respectable [rispéktəbəl] a. 존경할 만한, 훌륭한
respect (n. 존경) + able (a. …할 만한, 받을 만한)

stoop to something idiom …할 만큼 비열해지다
If you stoop to something, you do something bad or unpleasant in order to gain an advantage for yourself.

decent [díːsənt] a. 적당한; (사회 기준에) 맞는; 점잖은
Decent is used to describe something which is considered to be of an acceptable standard or quality.

scrape [skreip] v. 긁어내다, 떼다; 문지르다; 스쳐 …에 상처를 내다; n. 긁음; 문지르는 소리
If you scrape something from a surface, you remove it, especially by pulling a sharp object over the surface.

soil [sɔil] n. 흙, 땅
Soil is the substance on the surface of the earth in which plants grow.

Fantastic Mr. Fox

- **brick** [brik] n. 벽돌; vt. 벽돌로 막다
  Bricks are rectangular blocks of baked clay used for building walls, which are usually red or brown.

- **block** [blɑk] vt. (길 등을) 막다, 방해하다; n. 덩어리, 블록
  If you block someone's way, you prevent them from going somewhere or entering a place by standing in front of them.

Build Your Vocabulary

15. Bean's Secret Cider Cellar

crumbly [krʌ́mbli] a. 부서지기 쉬운, 푸석푸석한
Something that is crumbly is easily broken into a lot of little pieces.

whisker [hwískər] n. (고양이·쥐 등의) 수염; 구레나룻
The whiskers of an animal such as a cat or a mouse are the long stiff hairs that grow near its mouth.

snap [snæp] v. 날카롭게[느닷없이] 말하다; 덥석 물다; 휙 잡다; 짤깍 소리 내다; n. 툭 소리 냄
If someone snaps at you, they speak to you in a sharp, unfriendly way.

saucy [sɔ́:si] a. 뻔뻔스런, 건방진; 쾌활한, 재치 있는
Someone or something that is saucy is improperly forward or bold.

beast [bi:st] n. 야수, 짐승; 짐승 같은 인간
You can refer to an animal as a beast, especially if it is a large, dangerous, or unusual one.

shriek [ʃri:k] v. 새된 소리를 지르다, 비명을 지르다; n. 비명
When someone shrieks, they make a short, very loud cry.

pitch [pitʃ] n. 경기장; (노점상인 등의) 고정 위치; v. 던지다; 처박다
A pitch is an area of ground that is marked out and used for playing a game.

brilliant [bríljənt] a. 훌륭한, 멋진; 빛나는, 찬란한
A brilliant person, idea, or performance is extremely clever or skilful.

hop [hap] v. 깡충 뛰다, 뛰어 오르다; n. 깡충깡충 뜀
If you hop, you move along by jumping.

gulp [gʌlp] n. 꿀꺽꿀꺽 마심; v. 꿀꺽꿀꺽 마시다; (긴장, 흥분으로) 꿀꺽 삼키다
A gulp of air, food, or drink, is a large amount of it that you swallow at once.

biggish [bígiʃ] a. 약간 큰, 큰 편인
Something that is biggish is fairly big.

Fantastic Mr. Fox

- **creep** [kri:p] v. (crept-crept) 살금살금 걷다, 기다; n. 포복
  If something creeps somewhere, it moves very slowly.

- **vast** [væst] a. 광대한, 거대한
  Something that is vast is extremely large.

- **damp** [dæmp] a. 축축한; n. 습기
  Something that is damp is slightly wet.

- **gloomy** [glú:mi] a. 어두운, 우울한
  If a place is gloomy, it is almost dark so that you cannot see very well.

- **cellar** [sélər] n. 지하 저장실
  A cellar is a room underneath a building, which is often used for storing things in.

- **turkey** [tə́:rki] n. [조류] 칠면조; 바보, 멍청이
  A turkey is a large bird that is kept on a farm for its meat.

- **gloom** [glu:m] n. 어둠침침함, 어둠, 그늘
  The gloom is a state of near darkness.

- **peer** [piər] vi. 응시하다, 자세히 보다; 희미하게 나타나다
  If you peer at something, you look at it very hard.

- **accustomed** [əkʌ́stəmd] a. (…에) 익숙해진, 길들여진
  When your eyes become accustomed to darkness or bright light, they adjust so that you start to be able to see things, after not being able to see properly at first.

- **jar** [dʒɑ:r] n. 항아리, 단지, 병
  A jar is a glass container with a lid that is used for storing food.

- **tremendous** [triméndəs] a. 거대한, 대단한, 엄청난, 무서운
  You use tremendous to emphasize how strong a feeling or quality is, or how large an amount is.

- **banquet** [bǽŋkwit] n. 연회
  A banquet is a grand formal dinner.

Build Your Vocabulary

sneak [sni:k] v. 살금살금 돌아다니다; 슬쩍 넣다[집다]; 고자질하다; n. 밀고자
If you sneak somewhere, you go there very quietly on foot, trying to avoid being seen or heard.

gasp [gæsp] v. (놀람 따위로) 숨이 막히다, 헐떡거리다; n. 헐떡거림
When you gasp, you take a short quick breath through your mouth, especially when you are surprised, shocked, or in pain.

fizzy [fízi] a. 쉬잇 하고 거품이 이는, 청량감이 드는
Fizzy drinks are drinks that contain small bubbles of carbon dioxide.

brew [bru:] vt. 양조하다, (혼합 음료를) 만들다
If you brew tea or coffee, you add boiling water to it to make a hot drink, and if it brews, it gradually develops flavor in the container in which it was made.

fiery [fáiəri] a. 불같은; 불의, 화염의
You can use fiery for emphasis when you are referring to bright colors such as red or orange.

liquor [líkər] n. 술, 독주
Strong alcoholic drinks such as whisky, vodka, and gin can be referred to as liquor.

boil [bɔil] ① v. 끓(이)다; 격분하다; n. 끓임, 삶음 ② n. 종기, 부스럼
When a hot liquid boils or when you boil it, bubbles appear in it and it starts to change into steam.

miraculous [mirǽkjələs] a. 기적적인, 초자연적인; 놀랄 만한
If you describe a good event as miraculous, you mean that it is very surprising and unexpected.

fabulous [fǽbjələs] a. 굉장한, 멋진; 믿어지지 않는; 전설적인
If you describe something as fabulous, you are emphasizing that you like it a lot or think that it is very good.

tilt [tilt] v. 기울(이)다; n. 경사, 기울기
If you tilt an object or if it tilts, it moves into a sloping position with one end or side higher than the other.

Fantastic Mr. Fox

- **gurgle** [gə́:rgəl] v. (물 따위가) 꼴꼴[콸콸] 소리 내다; 옹알거리다
  If water is gurgling, it is making the sound that it makes when it flows quickly and unevenly through a narrow space.

- **sunbeam** [sʌ́nbìːm] n. 태양광선; 햇살, 일광
  A sunbeam is a ray of sunlight.

- **poach** [poutʃ] v. (남의 권리 등을) 가로채다; 밀렵하다
  If someone poaches fish, animals, or birds, they illegally catch them on someone else's property.

- **perch** [pəːrtʃ] v. (높은 곳에) 앉(히)다, 놓다
  If you perch on something, you sit down lightly on the very edge or tip of it.

- **rubber** [rʌ́bər] a. 고무의; n. 고무
  Rubber is a strong, waterproof, elastic substance made from the juice of a tropical tree or produced chemically.

- **insert** [insə́ːrt] vt. 끼워 넣다, 삽입하다, 넣다 (inserted a. 끼워 넣은)
  If you insert an object into something, you put the object inside it.

- **suck** [sʌk] v. 빨다, 흡수하다; n. 빨아들임
  If you suck something, you hold it in your mouth and pull at it with the muscles in your cheeks and tongue, for example in order to get liquid out of it.

- **clumsy** [klʌ́mzi] a. 서투른, 꼴사나운, 어색한
  A clumsy person moves or handles things in a careless, awkward way, often so that things are knocked over or broken.

- **brute** [bruːt] n. 짐승, 야만인; a. 잔인한, 야만적인; 무정한
  If you call someone, usually a man, a brute, you mean that they are rough, violent, and insensitive.

- **mess** [mes] v. 망쳐놓다, 방해하다; n. 난잡함, 엉망진창
  If you mess about, you spend time doing things without any particular purpose or without achieving anything.

Build Your Vocabulary

- **sip** [sip] v. 찔끔찔끔 마시다; n. 한 모금
  If you sip a drink or sip at it, you drink by taking just a small amount at a time.

- **freeze** [fri:z] v. (froze-frozen) 얼다, 얼어붙다; n. 결빙
  If someone who is moving freezes, they suddenly stop and become completely still and quiet.

- **prick (up) one's ears** idiom 귀를 쫑긋 세우다; 열심히 듣다
  If an animal pricks its ears, it raises them to listen to a sound.

Fantastic Mr. Fox

16. The Woman

row [rou] ① n. 열, 줄; 좌석 줄 ② v. (노를 써서) 배를 젓다
A row of things or people is a number of them arranged in a line.

peep [piːp] n. 엿봄, 훔쳐보기, 슬쩍 봄; vi. 엿보다, 슬쩍 들여다보다
A peep is a quick look at something, often secretly and quietly.

crack [kræk] n. 갈라진 금; 갑작스런 날카로운 소리; v. 찰칵 소리내다; 금이 가다; 깨다, 부수다
A crack is a very narrow gap between two things, or between two parts of a thing.

rolling-pin [róuliŋpin] n. (반죽을 미는) 밀방망이
A rolling-pin is a cylinder that you roll backwards and forwards over uncooked pastry in order to make the pastry flat.

bound [baund] ① a. 꼭 … 하게 되어 있는; 묶인; v. BIND의 과거·과거분사
② n. 경계, 범위 ③ v. 뛰어가다; 튀어 오르다; n. 튐, 반동
If you are bound by something such as a rule, agreement, or restriction, you are forced or required to act in a certain way.

rotten [rátn] a. 타락한, 부패한; 썩은
If you describe something as rotten, you think it is very unpleasant or of very poor quality.

string up phrasal v. 목매달아 죽이다, 교수형에 처하다
To string someone up means to kill them by hanging them.

porch [pɔːrtʃ] n. (본건물에서 달아낸 지붕 딸린) 현관
A porch is a sheltered area at the entrance to a building. It has a roof and sometimes has walls.

souvenir [sùːvəníər] n. 기념품
A souvenir is something which you buy or keep to remind you of a holiday, place, or event.

ruin [rúːin] v. 망치다, 못쓰게 만들다; 몰락하다; n. 폐허; 파멸
To ruin something means to severely harm, damage, or spoil it.

Build Your Vocabulary

- **stuff** [stʌf] vt. 채워 넣다, 속을 채우다; n. 물건, 물질
  If you stuff a container or space with something, you fill it with something or with a quantity of things until it is full.

- **quiver** [kwívər] v. (떨리듯) 흔들리다, 떨(리)다; n. 떨기
  If something quivers, it shakes with very small movements.

- **tuck** [tʌk] v. 밀어 넣다, 쑤셔 넣다; n. 접어 넣은 단
  If you tuck something somewhere, you put it there so that it is safe, comfortable, or neat.

- **sniff** [snif] v. 코를 킁킁거리다, 냄새를 맡다; 콧방귀를 뀌다; n. 킁킁거리며 냄새 맡음; 콧방귀 뀜
  When you sniff, you breathe in air through your nose to smell something.

- **poison** [pɔ́izən] vt. 독을 넣다[바르다]; 독살하다; n. 독, 독극물
  If someone poisons a food, drink, or weapon, they add poison to it so that it can be used to kill someone.

- **slam** [slæm] v. (문 따위를) 탕 닫(히)다, 세게 치다; 털썩 내려놓다; n. 쾅 (하는 소리)
  If you slam a door or window or if it slams, it shuts noisily and with great force.

- **shriek** [ʃriːk] v. 새된 소리를 지르다, 비명을 지르다; n. 비명
  When someone shrieks, they make a short, very loud cry.

- **nab** [næb] v. (특히 현행범을) 잡다, 체포하다; 움켜쥐다; n. 경찰; 체포
  If people in authority such as the police nab someone who they think has done something wrong, they catch them or arrest them.

- **poppycock** [pápikàk] n. 무의미, 허튼 소리, 난센스
  Poppycock is foolish talk.

- **clutch** [klʌtʃ] v. 꽉 잡다, 붙들다, 부여잡다; n. 붙잡음, 움켜쥠
  If you clutch at something or clutch something, you hold it tightly, usually because you are afraid or anxious.

- **gallon** [gǽlən] n. 갤런 (용량의 단위)
  A gallon is a unit of measurement for liquids that is equal to eight pints.

robber [rɑ́bər] n. 강도, 도둑
A robber is someone who steals money or property from a bank, a shop, or a vehicle, often by using force or threats.

bandit [bǽndit] n. 산적, 도둑; 악당, 무법자
Robbers are sometimes called bandits, especially if they are found in areas where the law has broken down.

burglar [bə́:rglər] n. (주거 침입) 강도
A burglar is a thief who enters a house or other building by force.

Build Your Vocabulary

17. The Great Feast

- **brick** [brik] vt. 벽돌로 막다; n. 벽돌
  If you brick up a hole, you close it with a wall of bricks.

- **glorious** [glɔ́ːriəs] a. 찬란한, 훌륭한, 영광스러운
  Something that is glorious is very beautiful and impressive.

- **cider** [sáidər] n. (영) 사과술
  Cider is a drink made from apples which in Britain usually contains alcohol.

- **impudent** [ímpjədənt] a. 뻔뻔스러운, 염치없는
  If you describe someone as impudent, you mean they are rude or disrespectful, or do something they have no right to do.

- **fellow** [félou] n. 친구, 동료
  You use fellow to describe people who are in the same situation as you, or people you feel you have something in common with.

- **feast** [fiːst] n. 축제; 대접; 진수성찬; v. 축연을 베풀다; 진수성찬을 먹다
  A feast is a large and special meal.

- **mighty** [máiti] a. 굉장한, 대단한, 강력한, 중대한
  Mighty is used to describe something that is very large or powerful.

- **glide** [glaid] v. 소리 없이 흘러가다, 미끄러지듯 움직이다; n. 활주, 활공
  If you glide somewhere, you move silently and in a smooth and effortless way.

- **bride** [braid] n. 신부
  A bride is a woman who is getting married or who has just got married.

- **hollow** [hálou] a. 속이 빈; 오목한; n. 구멍; 움푹한 곳; v. 속이 비다
  If you describe a statement, situation, or person as hollow, you mean they have no real value, worth, or effectiveness.

- **swallow** [swálou] v. (꿀꺽) 삼키다, 들이켜다; 싸다, 덮다; n. 삼킴, 마심
  If you swallow, you make a movement in your throat as if you are swallowing something, often because you are nervous or frightened.

Fantastic Mr. Fox

burst [bə:rst] v. 갑자기 …하다; 파열하다, 터지다; n. 파열, 돌발
If you say that something bursts into a particular situation or state, you mean that it suddenly changes into that situation or state.

goose [gu:s] n. (pl. geese) 거위
A goose is a large bird that has a long neck and webbed feet. Geese are often farmed for their meat.

amid [əmíd] prep. …의 한복판에; …이 한창일 때에
If something happens amid noises or events of some kind, it happens while the other things are happening.

ravenous [rǽvənəs] a. 몹시 굶주린; 게걸스럽게 먹는
If you are ravenous, you are extremely hungry.

crunch [krʌntʃ] v. 우두둑 깨물다[부수다]; n. 우두둑 부서지는 소리
If you crunch something hard, such as a sweet, you crush it noisily between your teeth.

succulent [sʌ́kjələnt] a. (과일 등이) 즙이 많은; 바람직한, 좋은
Succulent food, especially meat or vegetables, is juicy and good to eat.

toast [toust] n. 건배, 축배; 건배의 인사; v. 건배하다
When you drink a toast to someone or something, you drink some wine or another alcoholic drink as a symbolic gesture.

clap [klæp] v. 박수를[손뼉을] 치다; 가볍게 치다[두드리다]
When you clap, you hit your hands together to show appreciation or attract attention.

belch [beltʃ] n. 트림 (소리); 폭발(음), 분출; v. 분출하다, 내뿜다; 트림을 하다
A belch is a sudden noise from throat because air has risen up from stomach.

messrs [mésərz] n. (= messieurs) (pl.) 제군, 여러분
You use Messrs before the names of two or more men as the plural of Mister.

courtesy [kɔ́:rtəsi] n. 호의; 예의(바름), 정중, 친절
If you refer to the courtesy of doing something, you are referring to a polite action.

Build Your Vocabulary

* **colossal** [kəlásəl] a. 엄청난, 어마어마한; 거대한
  If you describe something as colossal, you are emphasizing that it is very large.

* **grin** [grin] v. 이를 드러내고 싱긋 웃다; n. 싱긋 웃음
  When you grin, you smile broadly.

* **yard** [jɑːrd] n. 야드(길이의 단위로 3피트 또는 0.9144미터에 해당); 마당, 뜰
  A yard is a unit for measuring length, equal to three feet or 0.91meters.

* **dig** [dig] v. 파다, 파헤치다; 찌르다; 탐구하다; n. 파기 (digger n. 땅 파는 사람[도구, 기계])
  If you dig one thing into another or if one thing digs into another, the first thing is pushed hard into the second, or presses hard into it.

* **set-up** [sétʌ̀p] n. (조직 등의) 구조, 구성
  A particular set-up is a particular system or way of organizing something.

* **buzz** [bʌz] n. 윙윙거리는 소리; v. 윙윙거리다; 분주하게 돌아다니다
  You can use buzz to refer to a long continuous sound, usually caused by lots of people talking at once.

* **marvellous** [máːrvələs] a. 훌륭한, 우수한; 놀라운, 믿기 어려운
  If you describe someone or something as marvellous, you are emphasizing that they are very good.

Fantastic Mr. Fox

18. Still Waiting

- **trickle** [tríkəl] vi. 똑똑 떨어지다, 졸졸 흐르다; (비밀 따위가) 조금씩 새어 나가다;
  n. 물방울, 실개울
  If liquid trickles somewhere, it flows slowly and without force in a thin line.

- **famish** [fǽmiʃ] vt. 굶주리게 하다 (famished a. 배가 고파 죽을 지경인)
  If you are famished, you are very hungry.

- **make a dash for** idiom …을 향해 돌진하다
  If you make a dash for a place, you run there very quickly, for example to escape from someone or something.

The Magic Finger

Comprehension Quiz

1. At the beginning of the story, Mr. Gregg loved _____.

  A. fishing

  B. hunting

  C. flying

  D. cooking

2. Why was the girl angry at Mr. Gregg and his sons?

  A. The boys didn't want to play a game.

  B. They killed a duck.

  C. They killed a deer.

  D. Mr. Gregg laughed at the girl.

3. The girl's teacher looked like a _____.

  A. cat

  B. mouse

  C. horse

  D. pig

4. Put the events in order: (–   –   –   –   –   )

   A. A flash comes from the girl's finger.

   B. Strange things happen to people.

   C. The girl gets angry.

   D. The girl feels hot.

   E. The flash touches the person who made her angry.

   F. The girl's finger tingles.

5. Mr. Gregg, William, and Phillip killed ___ ducks.

   A. 4

   B. 8

   C. 16

   D. 20

Comprehension Quiz

6. After the Magic Finger touched the Greggs, their bodies got small and they had _____.

   A. beaks

   B. duck bodies

   C. duck heads and feet

   D. wings

7. Put the events in order: (–   –   –   –   )

   A. Mr. and Mrs. Gregg flew.

   B. Mr. Gregg built a nest.

   C. Phillip and William flew.

   D. The big ducks went into the house.

   E. The Greggs got wings.

8. The big ducks did NOT _____.

   A. hold Mr. Gregg's gun

   B. play with Philip's train

   C. cook in the kitchen

   D. jump on William's bed

The Magic Finger

9. Why didn't the Greggs go inside their house at night?

　A. They couldn't open the door.

　B. They couldn't find their house.

　C. The ducks were inside their house.

　D. The door was locked.

10. The Greggs ate a few bites of _____.

　A. apples

　B. wormburgers

　C. seeds

　D. biscuits

Comprehension Quiz

11. When the girl called the Gregg's house, _____.

　A. she heard Phillip and William laughing

　B. she heard quacking

　C. nobody answered the phone

　D. she laughed at the Greggs

12. How was the weather at night?

　A. It rained.

　B. It snowed.

　C. It was very cold.

　D. It was nice and warm.

13. Mr. Gregg promised to _____.

　A. only hunt deer

　B. feed the ducks everyday

　C. plant flowers for the birds

　D. never hunt again

14. At the end of the story:

1. Mr. Gregg···	A. ran after Mr. Cooper.
2. Mrs. Gregg···	B. broke the guns.
3. Phillip and William···	C. put flowers on the ducks' graves.
4. The girl···	D. fed the birds.

The Magic Finger

15. Put the events in order: (–   –   –   –   –)

A. The ducks pointed guns at the Greggs.

B. The ducks flew back to the lake in the woods.

C. The ducks went inside the Gregg's house.

D. Mr. Gregg and his sons shot at the ducks.

E. The ducks flew over the Gregg's house.

F. The Greggs grew wings.

Build Your Vocabulary

- **own** [oun] vt. 소유하다, 지배하다; a. 자신의, 고유한
  If you own something, it is your property.

- **hunt** [hʌnt] v. 사냥하다, 추적하다; n. 사냥
  If you hunt for something or someone, you try to find them by searching carefully or thoroughly.

- **stand** [stænd] vi. 참다, 견디다; 서다, 일어서다
  If you cannot stand something, you cannot bear it or tolerate it.

- **deer** [diər] n. 사슴
  A deer is a large wild animal that eats grass and leaves.

- **cross** [krɔːs] a. 기분이 언짢은, 화가 나는; 교차한, 가로지른; n. 십자가; v. 가로지르다
  Someone who is cross is rather angry or irritated.

make faces (at somebody) idiom 얼굴을 찌푸리다
If you make faces, you produce an expression on your face to show that you do not like someone or something.

mind one's P's and Q's idiom 언행에 신경을 쓰다, 언행을 조심하다
If you are careful about the way you behave and are polite, you mind Your P's and Q's.

- **whisker** [hwískər] n. (고양이·쥐 등의) 수염; 구레나룻
  The whiskers of an animal such as a cat or a mouse are the long stiff hairs that grow near its mouth.

- **scream** [skriːm] v. 비명을 지르다; 소리치다; n. 비명
  When someone screams, they make a very loud, high-pitched cry, because they are in pain or are very frightened.

- **blackboard** [blǽkbɔ̀ːrd] n. 칠판
  A blackboard is a dark-colored board that you can write on with chalk.

- **bushy** [búʃi] a. 숱이 많은; 무성한, 우거진
  Bushy hair or fur is very thick.

The Magic Finger

- **wonder** [wʌ́ndər] v. 호기심을 가지다, 이상하게 여기다; n. 경탄할 만한 것, 경이
  If you wonder about something, you think about it because it interests you and you want to know more about it.

- **tip** [tip] ① n. 끝, 첨단 ② v. 기울(이)다, 뒤집어엎다 ③ n. 팁, 사례금
  The tip of something long and narrow is the end of it.

- **forefinger** [fɔ́ːrfìŋgər] n. 집게손가락
  Your forefinger is the finger that is next to your thumb.

- **tingle** [tíŋgəl] v. 따끔따끔 아프다, 쑤시다; 설레게 하다, 흥분시키다
  When a part of your body tingles, you have a slight stinging feeling there.

- **terribly** [térəbli] ad. 무섭게, 지독하게
  You use terribly to emphasize the great extent or degree of something.

- **sort** [sɔːrt] n. 종류, 부류; vt. 분류하다, 골라내다
  If you talk about a particular sort of something, you are talking about a class of things that have particular features in common and that belong to a larger group of related things.

- **electric** [iléktrik] a. 전기의; 전기를 이용하는
  An electric device works by means of electricity, rather than using some other source of power.

- **lake** [leik] n. 호수
  A large area of water that is surrounded by land.

- **beside oneself** idiom (격정·흥분으로) 이성을 잃고, 자신을 잊고, 어찌할 바를 모르고
  If you are beside yourself, you are unable to control yourself because of the strength of emotion you are feeling.

- **miss** [mis] vt. 놓치다, 빗맞히다
  If you miss something, you fail to hit, catch, reach, etc. something.

- **on earth** idiom [의문사를 강조하여] 도대체, 어떻게
  You use 'on earth' with questions, in order to express your surprise or anger.

- **be off** idiom [명령문] 꺼져; 떠나다, 출발하다
  If you say 'be off' to someone, you order them to leave the place immediately.

Build Your Vocabulary

* **yard** [jɑːrd] n. 마당, 뜰; 야드(길이의 단위)
A yard is a flat area of concrete or stone that is next to a building and often has a wall around it.

* **still** [stil] a. 조용한, 고요한; 정지한, 움직이지 않는; ad. 여전히, 아직도
If a place is still, it is quiet and shows no sign of activity.

* **firewood** [fáiərwùd] n. 장작, 땔나무
Firewood is wood that has been cut into pieces so that it can be burned on a fire.

* **yell** [jel] n. 고함소리, 부르짖음; v. 소리치다, 고함치다
A yell is a loud shout given by someone who is afraid or in pain.

* **tiny** [táini] a. 몹시 작은
Something or someone that is tiny is extremely small.

* **purple** [pə́ːrpəl] a. 자줏빛의; n. 자줏빛
Something that is purple is of a reddish-blue color.

* **sob** [sɑb] vi. 흐느껴 울다, 흐느끼다
If you sob something, you say it while you are crying.

* **witch** [witʃ] n. 마녀
In fairy stories, a witch is a woman, usually an old woman, who has evil magic powers.

* **flap** [flæp] v. 펄럭이게 하다, 휘날리다, 퍼덕이다; n. 펄럭임, 퍼덕거림
If a bird or insect flaps its wings or if its wings flap, the wings move quickly up and down.

* **burst** [bəːrst] v. 갑자기 …하다, 파열하다, 터지다; n. 파열, 돌발
(burst in phrasal v. 갑자기 들어오다)
If you burst in a room or building, you enter suddenly and noisily.

* **robin** [rábin] n. 유럽울새, 로빈
A robin is a small brown bird found in Europe.

chirrup [tʃírəp] v. 지저귀다
If a person or bird chirrups, they make short high-pitched sounds.

The Magic Finger

- **flown** [floun] v. fly(날다)의 과거분사 (fly–flew–flown)
  Flown is the past participle of fly.

- **enormous** [inɔ́ːrməs] a. 막대한, 거대한
  Something that is enormous is extremely large in size or amount.

  in a line idiom 한 줄로, 정렬하여, 일렬로
  If a group of people walk in a line, they walk in a position that forms a straight line.

- **swing** [swiŋ] v. 흔들다, 회전시키다
  If something swings or if you swing it, it moves repeatedly backwards and forwards or from side to side from a fixed point.

- **beak** [biːk] n. 새의 부리
  A bird's beak is the hard curved or pointed part of its mouth.

- **quack** [kwæk] vi. 꽥꽥 울다; 시끄럽게 지껄이다
  When a duck quacks, it makes the noise that ducks typically make.

- **nest** [nest] n. 둥지; 보금자리
  A bird's nest is the home that it makes to lay its eggs in.

- **stick** [stik] n. 나뭇가지; v. 찔리다; 달라붙다, 고착되다
  A stick is a thin branch which has fallen off a tree.

- **leaf** [liːf] n. (pl. leaves) 잎, 한 장
  The leaves of a tree or plant are the parts that are flat, thin, and usually green.

- **feather** [féðər] n. 깃털, 깃
  A bird's feathers are the soft covering on its body.

  on and on idiom 쉬지 않고, 계속해서
  If something happens on and on, it happens without stopping.

- **hop** [hɑp] v. 뛰다, 깡충 뛰다, 뛰어 오르다
  If you hop, you move along by jumping on one foot.

- **lay** [lei] v. (알을) 낳다; 놓다, 두다
  When a female bird lays an egg, it produces an egg by pushing it out of its body.

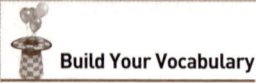

Build Your Vocabulary

tin [tin] n. 주석; 깡통; 통조림
A tin is a metal container which is filled with food and sealed in order to preserve the food for long periods of time.

biscuit [bískit] n. 비스킷
A biscuit is a small flat cake that is crisp and usually sweet.

peck [pek] v. 쪼다, 쪼아 먹다
When a bird pecks, it bites, hits or picks up something small with its beak.

bit [bit] n. 작은 조각, 한 조각; 조금, 약간
A bit of something is a small piece of it.

beastly [bíːstli] a. 짐승 같은, 더러운, 추잡한
If you describe something as beastly, you mean that it is very unpleasant.

stove [stouv] n. (요리용) 화로; 스토브, 난로; v. 난로로 데우다
A stove is a piece of equipment which provides heat, either for cooking or for heating a room.

dare [dɛər] v. 감히 …하다; 무릅쓰다; 도전하다
If you dare to do something, you do something which requires a lot of courage.

take over idiom 차지하다, 탈취하다, 인수하다
If someone takes over a country or building, they get control of it by force.

worm [wəːrm] n. 벌레
A worm is a small animal with a long thin body, no bones and no legs.

slug [slʌg] n. 민달팽이
A slug is a small slow-moving creature with a long soft body and no legs, like a snail without a shell.

hug [hʌg] v. 꼭 껴안다; n. 포옹
When you hug someone, you put your arms around them and hold them tightly.

mince [mins] vt. (고기 따위를) 다지다, 잘게 썰다
If you mince food such as meat, you put it into a machine which cuts it into very small pieces.

The Magic Finger

slugburger n. 민달팽이 버거. 저자가 합성한 단어
slug(n. 민달팽이) + burger(n. 버거)

wormburger n. 벌레 버거. 저자가 합성한 단어
worm(n. 벌레) + burger(n. 버거)

disgust [disgʌ́st] vt. 역겹게 하다, 넌더리나게 하다 (disgusting a. 메스꺼운, 역겨운)
If you say that something is disgusting, you mean that you find it completely unacceptable.

blow [blou] v. (blew-blown) 불다, 바람에 날리다; n. 불기; 강타, 타격
When a wind or breeze blows, the air moves.

rock [rɑk] v. 흔들다, 흔들리다, 요동치다; n. 바위, 암석
When something rocks or when you rock it, it moves slowly and regularly backwards and forwards or from side to side.

wet [wet] a. 젖은, 축축한
If something is wet, it is covered in water, rain, sweat, tears, or another liquid.

peep [pi:p] vi. 엿보다, 슬쩍 보다
If you peep, or peep at something, you have a quick look at it, often secretly and quietly.

throw away idiom 버리다, 없애다
When you throw away something that you do not want, you get rid of it.

congratulate [kəngrǽtʃəlèit] vt. 축하하다
If you congratulate someone, you say something to show you are pleased that something nice has happened to them.

admit [ædmít] v. 인정하다
If you admit that something bad, unpleasant, or embarrassing is true, you agree, often unwillingly, that it is true.

stare [stɛər] v. 응시하다, 뚫어지게 보다
If you stare at someone or something, you look at them for a long time.

queer [kwiər] a. 별난, 기묘한, 이상한
Something that is queer is strange.

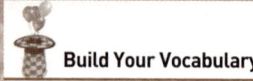

Build Your Vocabulary

- **smash** [smæʃ] v. 때려 부수다, 깨뜨리다
  If you smash something or if it smashes, it breaks into many pieces.

- **piece** [piːs] n. 조각, 단편, 파편, 일부분
  A piece of something is an amount of it that has been broken off, torn off, or cut off.

- **hammer** [hǽmər] n. 망치, 해머; v. (망치로) 두들겨 펴다
  A hammer is a tool with a handle and a heavy metal head, used for breaking things or hitting nails.

- **mound** [maund] n. 흙더미, 언덕
  A mound of something is a large rounded pile of it.

- **soil** [sɔil] n. 흙, 땅, 지면; v. 더럽히다
  Soil is the substance on the surface of the earth in which plants grow.

- **grave** [greiv] n. 무덤, 묘
  A grave is a place where a dead person is buried.

- **sack** [sæk] n. 마대, 자루
  A sack is a large bag, especially one made of coarse cloth or paper.

- **barley** [báːrli] n. 보리, 대맥
  Barley is a grain that is used to make food, beer, and whisky.

- **dove** [douv] n. 비둘기 (pigeon보다 작고 밝은 색의 비둘기)
  A dove is a bird that looks like pigeon but is smaller and lighter in color.

- **pigeon** [pídʒən] n. 비둘기 (dove보다 크고 회색 빛깔의 비둘기)
  A pigeon is a bird, usually grey in color, which has a fat body.

- **sparrow** [spǽrou] n. 참새
  A sparrow is a small brown bird that is very common in Britain.

- **lark** [laːrk] n. 종달새
  A lark is a small brown bird which makes a pleasant sound.

The Magic Finger

scatter [skǽtər] v. 흩뿌리다, 뿌리다
If you scatter things over an area, you throw or drop them so that they spread all over the area.

handful [hǽndfùl] n. 한 움큼, 손에 그득, 한 줌
A handful of something is the amount of it that you can hold in your hand.

lower [lóuər] v. 낮추다, 내리다
If you lower something, you move it slowly downwards.

in hono(u)r of idiom ⋯에 경의를 표하여
If something is arranged in hono(u)r of a particular event, it is arranged in order to celebrate that event.

dotty [dáti] a. (구어) 머리가 돈
If you say that someone is dotty, you mean that they are slightly mad or likely to do strange things.

proud [praud] a. 자부심이 있는, 긍지를 가진 (proudly ad. 자랑스럽게)
If you feel proud, you feel pleased about something good that you possess or have done.

bathroom [bǽθrù(:)m] n. 화장실, 욕실
A bathroom is a room in a house that contains a bath or shower, a wash-basin, and sometimes a toilet.

mess [mes] n. 난잡함, 뒤죽박죽, 엉망; v. 어질러놓다, 더럽히다, 망쳐놓다
If you say that something is a mess, you think that it is in an untidy state.

tub [tʌb] n. 통, 물통; 욕조, 목욕통
A tub is the same as a bathtub. A bathtub is a long, usually rectangular container which you fill with water and sit in to wash your body.

brim [brim] n. 가장자리; 테두리; (모자의) 챙
The brim of a hat is the wide part that sticks outwards at the bottom.

Comprehension Quiz Answers

The Enormous Crocodile
1. C
2. A, D
3. B
4. A
5. C
6. D
7. D
8. C
9. A, B
10. B
11. D
12. B
13. D
14. B
15. B
16. A, C
17. D
18. B
19. D
20. D
21. A
22. B, D
23. D
24. B
25. C
26. D
27. A, C
28. A-C-B-D
29. C
30. C-D-A-B

The Giraffe and the Pelly and Me
1. B
2. B
3. A
4. C
5. B-E-D-A-C
6. D-C-E-A-B
7. B
8. B
9. D
10. B
11. A
12. C
13. B
14. A-C-B-E-D
15. 1-B, 2-E, 3-A, 4-C, 5-D
16. 1-D, 2-B, 3-A, 4-E, 5-C
17. C
18. D-A-E-B-C
19. A
20. C
21. D
22. C
23. A
24. C
25. A
26. C
27. 1-C, 2-A, 3-B
28. C
29. 1-B, 2-D, 3-C, 4-A
30. D
31. C
32. B
33. B-A-C-D-E
34. 1-D, 2-C, 3-A, 4-B
35. 1-B, 2-D, 3-A, 4-C

Fantastic Mr. Fox
Chapters 1 and 2
1. B
2. C
3. B
4. A
5. C

Chapters 3 and 4
1. D
2. D-A-B-E-C
3. A
4. B
5. D

Chapters 5 and 6
1. B
2. B
3. A
4. D-A-E-B-C
5. 1-B, 2-E, 3-A, 4-C, 5-D

Chapters 7 and 8
1. B-E-D-C-A
2. 1-C, 2-D, 3-B, 4-A
3. A
4. C
5. B

Chapters 9 and 10
1. 1-B, 2-D, 3-A, 4-C
2. B
3. A-C-E-D-B
4. B
5. A

Chapters 11 and 12
1. B
2. A
3. 1-B, 2-E, 3-A, 4-C, 5-D
4. B
5. C

Chapters 13 and 14
1. A
2. C
3. D
4. E-A-C-D-B
5. C

Chapters 15 and 16
1. A
2. B
3. D
4. B
5. 1-B, 2-D, 3-A, 4-C

Chapters 17 and 18
1. D
2. 1-B, 2-D, 3-A, 4-C
3. C-E-A-D-B
4. C
5. 1-C, 2-D, 3-E, 4-B, 5-A

The Magic Finger
1. B
2. C
3. A
4. C-D-F-A-E-B
5. C
6. D
7. E-C-A-D-B
8. D
9. C
10. A
11. B
12. A
13. D
14. 1-B, 2-C, 3-D, 4-A
15. D-E-F-C-A-B

영어원서 읽기 Tips

Roald Dahl Short Stories를 완독하셨군요! 축하합니다!

원서 읽는 단어장을 활용해보세요!

다양한 원서들을 「원서 읽는 단어장」을 활용해서 읽어보세요. 「Charlie and the Chocolate Factory」를 비롯한 로알드 달의 작품들과 「Twilight」, 「New Moon」, 「Harry Potter and the Sorcerer's Stone」 등 여러 영어원서의 단어장이 출간되어 있습니다. 「원서 읽는 단어장」은 시중 서점 및 인터넷 서점에서 구입할 수 있습니다.

인터넷 서점에서 '원서 읽는 단어장'을 검색해보세요!

「원서 읽는 단어장」 시리즈

- Charlie and the Chocolate Factory
- Matilda
- James and the Giant Peach
- Shopaholic
- Frindle
- The Secret
- Twilight
- Harry Potter and the Sorcerer's Stone
- Charlotte's Web
- New Moon

함께 모여 원서 읽는 〈스피드 리딩 카페〉

함께 모여 원서를 읽는 〈스피드 리딩 카페〉(cafe.naver.com/readingtc)를 방문해보세요. '수준별 추천 원서 목록', '함께 만든 원서별 단어장', '매월 진행되는 북클럽' 등 원서 읽기에 도움이 되는 자료가 넘쳐납니다. 무엇보다 원서를 함께 읽을 수천 명의 동료들을 만날 수 있는 멋진 곳입니다. 원서 읽기에 관심이 있으시다면 이곳을 방문해서 함께 참여해보세요!

**많은 글을 읽는 것은 영어를 익히는 가장 좋은 방법이 아니다.
그것은 '유일한' 방법이다.** – 세계적인 언어학자 스티븐 크라센 교수

영어원서 읽기는 모두가 인정하는 최고의 영어 공부법입니다. 일상에서 영어를 사용하지 않는 비영어권 국가에서 영어에 가장 쉽고, 편하고, 저렴하게 노출되는 방법이 '원서 읽기'이기 때문입니다. 하지만 영어 구사력이 뛰어나지 않은 한국의 보통 영어 학습자들에게는 선뜻 시작하기 부담스러운 것도 사실입니다. 이런 학습자들을 위하여 영어 초보자들도 쉽게 원서 읽기를 시작하고, 꾸준한 읽기를 통해 '영어원서 읽기 습관'을 만들 수 있도록 고안된 책을 소개합니다.

● 각 도서는 해당 영화의 소설판 영어원서입니다.

인터넷 서점에서 '영화로 읽는 영어원서'를 검색해보세요!

출간된 본 시리즈 도서들은 독자들의 큰 사랑을 받으며 어학 분야의 베스트셀러를 기록했고, 학원과 학교들에서도 꾸준히 교재로 채택되는 등 영어 학습자들에게 좋은 반응을 얻고 있습니다. (EBS가 운영하는 어학 사이트 EBSlang(www.ebslang.co.kr), 서초·강남 등지 명문 중고교 방과 후 보충 교재 채택 등)

Text copyright © 2010 Longtail Books
Illustrations © 2010 Quentin Blake

이 책에 사용된 일러스트 사용 권한은 AP Watt Ltd.를 통해 계약한 롱테일북스에 있습니다.
한국 내에서 보호받는 저작물이므로 무단 전재와 무단 복제를 금합니다.

원서 읽는 단어장
Roald Dahl Short Stories

1판 1쇄 2010년 11월 1일
1판 11쇄 2024년 9월 30일

기획 이수영
책임편집 김보경 유난영
콘텐츠 제작 롱테일 교육 연구소
마케팅 두잉글 사업 본부

펴낸이 이수영
펴낸곳 롱테일북스
출판등록 제2015-000191호
주소 04033 서울특별시 마포구 양화로 113, 3층(서교동, 순흥빌딩)
전자메일 help@ltinc.net

ISBN 978-89-5605-487-2 14740
    978-89-5605-319-6 (세트)